Wild·Animals·Have·KnowN

·and·200·Drawings·

by

Ernest Thompson Seton

Being the Personal Histories of
Lobo
Silverspot
Rappylup
Bingo
The Springfield Fox
The Pacing Mustang
Wully
and Redruff

DOVER PUBLICATIONS, INC.
Mineola, New York

Published in Canada by General Publishing Company, Ltd., 30 Lesmill Road, Don Mills, Toronto, Ontario.

Bibliographical Note

This Dover edition, first published in 2000, is an unabridged republication of a standard edition of *Wild Animals I Have Known,* originally published by Charles Scribner's Sons, New York, in 1898, under the author's name of Ernest Seton Thompson.

Library of Congress Cataloging-in-Publication Data

Seton, Ernest Thompson, 1860–1946.
 Wild animals I have known / Ernest Thompson Seton. — Dover ed.
  p. cm.
 Originally published: New York : Charles Scribner's Sons, 1898.
 ISBN 0-486-41084-6 (pbk.)
  1. Animals. I. Title.

QL791 .S52 2000
599—dc21
                                                99-055706

Manufactured in the United States of America
Dover Publications, Inc., 31 East 2nd Street, Mineola, N.Y. 11501

This Book
is Dedicated

To Jim

Nouna S.

A List of the Stories in this Book

Note to the Reader

THESE STORIES are true. Although I have left the strict line of historical truth in many places, the animals in this book were all real characters. They lived the lives I have depicted, and showed the stamp of heroism and personality more strongly by far than it has been in the power of my pen to tell.

I believe that natural history has lost much by the vague general treatment that is so common. What satisfaction would be derived from a ten-page sketch of the habits and customs of Man ? How much more profitable it would be to devote that space to the life of some one great man. This is the principle I have endeavored to apply to my animals. The real personality of the individual, and his view of life are my theme, rather than the ways of the

Note to the Reader

race in general, as viewed by a casual and hostile human eye.

This may sound inconsistent in view of my having pieced together some of the characters, but that was made necessary by the fragmentary nature of the records. There is, however, almost no deviation from the truth in Lobo, Bingo, and the Mustang.

Lobo lived his wild romantic life from 1889 to 1894 in the Currumpaw region, as the ranchmen know too well, and died, precisely as related, on January 31, 1894.

Bingo was my dog from 1882 to 1888, in spite of interruptions, caused by lengthy visits to New York, as my Manitoban friends will remember. And my old friend, the owner of Tan, will learn from these pages how his dog really died.

The Mustang lived not far from Lobo in the early nineties. The story is given strictly as it occurred, excepting that there is a dispute as to the manner of his death. According to some testimony he broke his neck in the corral that

Note to the Reader

he was first taken to. Old Turkeytrack is where
he cannot be consulted to settle it.

Wully is, in a sense, a compound of two dogs;
both were mongrels, of some collie blood, and
were raised as sheep-dogs. The first part of
Wully is given as it happened, after that it was
known only that he became a savage, treacherous sheep-killer. The details of the second part
belong really to another, a similar yaller dog,
who long lived the double life—a faithful sheep-
dog by day, and a bloodthirsty, treacherous
monster by night. Such things are less rare
than is supposed, and since writing these stories
I have heard of another double-lived sheep-dog
that added to its night amusements the crown-
ing barbarity of murdering the smaller dogs of
the neighborhood. He had killed twenty and
hidden them in a sand-pit, when discovered by
his master. He died just as Wully did.

About 1904, while at Salt Lake City, I met an
old cattleman who gave me new light on the
Pacing Mustang. He told me that he was one
of the boys who tried to run the Pacer down.

9

Note to the Reader

Also, that he was present at the final scene. This cattleman claimed that Old Turkeytrack did get the Pacer into the corral, but found him so ferociously unmanageable that the horseman shouted out: "Throw open that gate." This done, the Pacer, with his rider, raced across the prairie. The man thought to wear the Pacer down, but suddenly, the horse dashed to the canyon, and leaped over the edge, taking his rider with him. Both were smashed together.

All told, I now have information of six of these Jekyl-Hyde dogs. In each case it happened to be a collie.

Many dogs have I known since the above was penned, and much that looks like treachery have I seen. Is it treachery? In the light of my larger experience, I should say not. The dog has always been the model and symbol of fidelity; and I have never known a dog that was false to the master that brought him up. In other words, the dog that played false, had changed masters; he did not know to whom his loyalty was due.

Note to the Reader

Redruff really lived in the Don Valley north of Toronto, and many of my companions will remember him. He was killed in 1889, between the Sugar Loaf and Castle Frank, by a creature whose name I have withheld, as it is the species, rather than the individual, that I wish to expose.

Silverspot, Raggylug, and Vixen are founded on real characters. Though I have ascribed to them the adventures of more than one of their kind, every incident in their biographies is from life.

The fact that these stories are true is the reason why all are tragic. The life of a wild animal *always has a tragic end.*

Such a collection of histories naturally suggests a common thought—a moral it would have been called in the last century. No doubt each different mind will find a moral to its taste, but I hope some will herein find emphasized a moral as old as Scripture—we and the beasts are kin. Man has nothing that the animals have not at least a vestige of, the animals have

11

Note to the Reader

nothing that man does not in some degree share.

Since, then, the animals are creatures with wants and feelings differing in degree only from our own, they surely have their rights. This fact, now beginning to be recognized by the Caucasian world, was first proclaimed by Moses and was emphasized by the Buddhist over two thousand years ago.

E. T. S.

Lobo
The King of Currumpaw

Lobo

The King of Currumpaw

I

URRUMPAW is a vast cattle range in northern New Mexico. It is a land of rich pastures and teeming flocks and herds, a land of rolling mesas and precious running waters that at length unite in the Currumpaw River, from which the whole region is named. And the king whose despotic power was felt over its entire extent was an old gray wolf.

Old Lobo, or the king, as the Mexicans called him, was the gigantic leader of a remarkable pack of gray wolves, that had ravaged the Currumpaw Valley for a number of years. All the shepherds and ranchmen knew him well, and, wherever he appeared with his trusty band, terror reigned supreme among the cattle, and wrath and despair among their owners. Old Lobo was a giant among wolves, and was cunning and strong in proportion to his size. His voice at night was well-known and easily distinguished from that of any of his fellows. An ordinary wolf might howl half the night about the herdsman's bivouac without attracting more than a passing notice, but when the deep roar of the old king came booming down the cañon, the watcher bestirred himself and prepared to learn in the morning that fresh and serious inroads had been made among the herds.

Old Lobo's band was but a small one. This I never quite understood, for usually, when a wolf rises to the position and power that he had, he attracts a numerous following. It may be that he had as many as he desired, or perhaps his ferocious temper prevented the increase of his pack. Certain is it that Lobo had only five followers during the latter part of his reign. Each of these, however, was a wolf of renown, most of them were above the ordinary size, one in particular, the second in command, was a

veritable giant, but even he was far below the
leader in size and prowess. Several of the band,
besides the two leaders, were especially noted.
One of those was a beautiful white wolf, that
the Mexicans called Blanca ; this was supposed
to be a female, possibly Lobo's mate. Another
was a yellow wolf of remarkable swiftness, which,
according to current stories had, on several occasions, captured an antelope for the pack.

It will be seen, then, that these wolves were
thoroughly well-known to the cowboys and
shepherds. They were frequently seen and
oftener heard, and their lives were intimately
associated with those of the cattlemen, who
would so gladly have destroyed them. There
was not a stockman on the Currumpaw who
would not readily have given the value of
many steers for the scalp of any one of Lobo's
band, but they seemed to possess charmed lives,
and defied all manner of devices to kill them.
They scorned all hunters, derided all poisons,
and continued, for at least five years, to exact
their tribute from the Currumpaw ranchers to
the extent, many said, of a cow each day. According to this estimate, therefore, the band had

killed more than two thousand of the finest stock, for, as was only too well-known, they selected the best in every instance.

The old idea that a wolf was constantly in a starving state, and therefore ready to eat anything, was as far as possible from the truth in this case, for these freebooters were always sleek and well-conditioned, and were in fact most fastidious about what they ate. Any animal that had died from natural causes, or that was diseased or tainted, they would not touch, and they even rejected anything that had been killed by the stockmen. Their choice and daily food was the tenderer part of a freshly killed yearling heifer. An old bull or cow they disdained, and though they occasionally took a young calf or colt, it was quite clear that veal or horseflesh was not their favorite diet. It was also known that they were not fond of mutton, although they often amused themselves by killing sheep. One night in November, 1893, Blanca and the yellow wolf killed two hundred and fifty sheep, apparently for the fun of it, and did not eat an ounce of their flesh.

Lobo

These are examples of many stories which I might repeat, to show the ravages of this destructive band. Many new devices for their extinction were tried each year, but still they lived and throve in spite of all the efforts of their foes. A great price was set on Lobo's head, and in consequence poison in a score of subtle forms was put out for him, but he never failed to detect and avoid it. One thing only he feared—that was firearms, and knowing full well that all men in this region carried them, he never was known to attack or face a human being. Indeed, the set policy of his band was to take refuge in flight whenever, in the daytime, a man was descried, no matter at what distance. Lobo's habit of permitting the pack to eat only that which they themselves had killed, was in numerous cases their salvation, and the keenness of his scent to detect the taint of human hands or the poison itself, completed their immunity.

On one occasion, one of the cowboys heard the too familiar rallying-cry of Old Lobo, and stealthily approaching, he found the Currumpaw pack in a hollow, where they had ' round-

ed up' a small herd of cattle. Lobo sat apart
on a knoll, while Blanca with the rest was endeavoring to 'cut out' a young cow, which
they had selected; but the cattle were standing
in a compact mass with their heads outward,
and presented to the foe a line of horns, unbroken save when some cow, frightened by a
fresh onset of the wolves, tried to retreat into
the middle of the herd. It was only by taking
advantage of these breaks that the wolves had
succeeded at all in wounding the selected cow,
but she was far from being disabled, and it
seemed that Lobo at length lost patience with
his followers, for he left his position on the hill,
and, uttering a deep roar, dashed toward the herd.
The terrified rank broke at his charge, and he
sprang in among them. Then the cattle scattered
like the pieces of a bursting bomb. Away went
the chosen victim, but ere she had gone twenty-
five yards Lobo was upon her. Seizing her by
the neck he suddenly held back with all his
force and so threw her heavily to the ground.
The shock must have been tremendous, for the
heifer was thrown heels over head. Lobo also
turned a somersault, but immediately recovered

himself, and his followers falling on the poor cow, killed her in a few seconds. Lobo took no part in the killing—after having thrown the victim, he seemed to say, " Now, why could not some of you have done that at once without wasting so much time?"

The man now rode up shouting, the wolves as usual retired, and he, having a bottle of strychnine, quickly poisoned the carcass in three places, then went away, knowing they would return to feed, as they had killed the animal themselves. But next morning, on going to look for his expected victims, he found that, although the wolves had eaten the heifer, they had carefully cut out and thrown aside all those parts that had been poisoned.

The dread of this great wolf spread yearly among the ranchmen, and each year a larger price was set on his head, until at last it reached $1,000, an unparalleled wolf-bounty, surely; many a good man has been hunted down for less. Tempted by the promised reward, a Texan ranger named Tannerey came one day galloping up the cañon of the Currumpaw. He had a superb outfit for wolf-hunting—the best

of guns and horses, and a pack of enormous wolf-hounds. Far out on the plains of the Pan-handle, he and his dogs had killed many a wolf, and now he never doubted that, within a few days, old Lobo's scalp would dangle at his saddle-bow.

Away they went bravely on their hunt in the gray dawn of a summer morning, and soon the great dogs gave joyous tongue to say that they were already on the track of their quarry. Within two miles, the grizzly band of Currumpaw leaped into view, and the chase grew fast and furious. The part of the wolf-hounds was merely to hold the wolves at bay till the hunter could ride up and shoot them, and this usually was easy on the open plains of Texas ; but here a new feature of the country came into play, and showed how well Lobo had chosen his range ; for the rocky cañons of the Currumpaw and its tributaries intersect the prairies in every direction. The old wolf at once made for the nearest of these and by crossing it got rid of the horsemen. His band then scattered and thereby scattered the dogs, and when they reunited at a distant point of course all of

the dogs did not turn up, and the wolves no longer outnumbered, turned on their pursuers and killed or desperately wounded them all. That night when Tannerey mustered his dogs, only six of them returned, and of these, two were terribly lacerated. This hunter made two other attempts to capture the royal scalp, but neither of them was more successful than the first, and on the last occasion his best horse met its death by a fall ; so he gave up the chase in disgust and went back to Texas, leaving Lobo more than ever the despot of the region.

Next year, two other hunters appeared, determined to win the promised bounty. Each believed he could destroy this noted wolf, the first by means of a newly devised poison, which was to be laid out in an entirely new manner ; the other a French Canadian, by poison assisted with certain spells and charms, for he firmly believed that Lobo was a veritable ' loup-garou,' and could not be killed by ordinary means. But cunningly compounded poisons, charms, and incantations were all of no avail against this grizzly devastator. He

23

made his weekly rounds and daily banquets as aforetime, and before many weeks had passed, Calone and Laloche gave up in despair and went elsewhere to hunt.

In the spring of 1893, after his unsuccessful attempt to capture Lobo, Joe Calone had a humiliating experience, which seems to show that the big wolf simply scorned his enemies, and had absolute confidence in himself. Calone's farm was on a small tributary of the Currumpaw, in a picturesque cañon, and among the rocks of this very cañon, within a thousand yards of the house, old Lobo and his mate selected their den and raised their family that season. There they lived all summer, and killed Joe's cattle, sheep, and dogs, but laughed at all his poisons and traps, and rested securely among the recesses of the cavernous cliffs, while Joe vainly racked his brain for some method of smoking them out, or of reaching them with dynamite. But they escaped entirely unscathed, and continued their ravages as before. "There's where he lived all last summer," said Joe, pointing to the face of the cliff, "and I couldn't do a thing with him. I was like a fool to him."

Lobo

II

THIS history, gathered so far from the cowboys, I found hard to believe until in the fall
of 1893, I made the acquaintance of the wily
marauder, and at length came to know him
more thoroughly than anyone else. Some
years before, in the Bingo days, I had been
a wolf-hunter, but my occupations since then
had been of another sort, chaining me to stool
and desk. I was much in need of a change,
and when a friend, who was also a ranch-owner
on the Currumpaw, asked me to come to New
Mexico and try if I could do anything with
this predatory pack, I accepted the invitation
and, eager to make the acquaintance of its
king, was as soon as possible among the mesas
of that region. I spent some time riding about
to learn the country, and at intervals, my guide
would point to the skeleton of a cow to which
the hide still adhered, and remark, "That's
some of his work."

It became quite clear to me that, in this
rough country, it was useless to think of pur-

suing Lobo with hounds and horses, so that poison or traps were the only available expedients. At present we had no traps large enough, so I set to work with poison.

I need not enter into the details of a hundred devices that I employed to circumvent this 'loup-garou'; there was no combination of strychnine, arsenic, cyanide, or prussic acid, that I did not essay; there was no manner of flesh that I did not try as bait; but morning after morning, as I rode forth to learn the result, I found that all my efforts had been useless. The old king was too cunning for me. A single instance will show his wonderful sagacity. Acting on the hint of an old trapper, I melted some cheese together with the kidney fat of a freshly killed heifer, stewing it in a china dish, and cutting it with a bone knife to avoid the taint of metal. When the mixture was cool, I cut it into lumps, and making a hole in one side of each lump, I inserted a large dose of strychnine and cyanide, contained in a capsule that was impermeable by any odor; finally I sealed the holes up with pieces of the cheese itself. During the whole process, I wore a

26

Lobo

pair of gloves steeped in the hot blood of the heifer, and even avoided breathing on the baits. When all was ready, I put them in a raw-hide bag rubbed all over with blood, and rode forth dragging the liver and kidneys of the beef at the end of a rope. With this I made a ten-mile circuit, dropping a bait at each quarter of a mile, and taking the utmost care, always, not to touch any with my hands.

Lobo, generally, came into this part of the range in the early part of each week, and passed the latter part, it was supposed, around the base of Sierra Grande. This was Monday, and that same evening, as we were about to retire, I heard the deep bass howl of his majesty. On hearing it one of the boys briefly remarked, "There he is, we'll see."

The next morning I went forth, eager to know the result. I soon came on the fresh trail of the robbers, with Lobo in the lead—his track was always easily distinguished. An ordinary wolf's forefoot is $4\frac{1}{2}$ inches long, that of a large wolf $4\frac{3}{4}$ inches, but Lobo's, as measured a number of times, was $5\frac{1}{2}$ inches from claw to heel; I afterward found that his

27

other proportions were commensurate, for he stood three feet high at the shoulder, and weighed 150 pounds. His trail, therefore, though obscured by those of his followers, was never difficult to trace. The pack had soon found the track of my drag, and as usual followed it. I could see that Lobo had come to the first bait, sniffed about it, and finally had picked it up.

Then I could not conceal my delight. "I've got him at last," I exclaimed; "I shall find him stark within a mile," and I galloped on with eager eyes fixed on the great broad track in the dust. It led me to the second bait and that also was gone. How I exulted—I surely have him now and perhaps several of his band. But there was the broad paw-mark still on the drag; and though I stood in the stirrup and scanned the plain I saw nothing that looked like a dead wolf. Again I followed—to find now that the third bait was gone—and the king-wolf's track led on to the fourth, there to learn that he had not really taken a bait at all, but had merely carried them in his mouth. Then having piled the three on the fourth, he

scattered filth over them to express his utter contempt for my devices. After this he left my drag and went about his business with the pack he guarded so effectively.

This is only one of many similar experiences which convinced me that poison would never avail to destroy this robber, and though I continued to use it while awaiting the arrival of the traps, it was only because it was meanwhile a sure means of killing many prairie wolves and other destructive vermin.

About this time there came under my observation an incident that will illustrate Lobo's diabolic cunning. These wolves had at least one pursuit which was merely an amusement, it was stampeding and killing sheep, though they rarely ate them. The sheep are usually kept in flocks of from one thousand to three thousand under one or more shepherds. At night they are gathered in the most sheltered place available, and a herdsman sleeps on each side of the flock to give additional protection. Sheep are such senseless creatures that they are liable to be stampeded by the veriest trifle, but they have deeply ingrained in their nature one, and perhaps only one, strong weakness, namely, to follow their leader. And this the shepherds turn to good account by putting half a dozen goats in the flock of sheep. The latter recognize the superior intelligence of their bearded cousins, and when a night alarm occurs they crowd around them, and usually are thus saved from a stampede and are easily protected. But it was not always so. One night late in last November, two Perico shepherds were aroused by an onset of wolves. Their flocks huddled  around the goats, which being neither fools nor cowards, stood their ground and were bravely defiant ; but alas for them, no common wolf was heading this attack. Old Lobo, the weir-wolf, knew as well as the shepherds that the goats were the moral force of the flock, so hastily running over the backs of the densely packed sheep, he fell on these leaders, slew them all in a few minutes, and soon had the luckless sheep stampeding in a thousand different directions. For weeks afterward I was almost daily accosted by some anxious shepherd, who asked, "Have you seen any stray OTO sheep lately?" and usually I was obliged to

Lobo

say I had ; one day it was, " Yes, I came on some five or six carcasses by Diamond Springs ;" or another, it was to the effect that I had seen a small ' bunch' running on the Malpai Mesa ; or again, " No, but Juan Meira saw about twenty, freshly killed, on the Cedra Monte two days ago."

At length the wolf traps arrived, and with two men I worked a whole week to get them properly set out. We spared no labor or pains, I adopted every device I could think of that might help to insure success. The second day after the traps arrived, I rode around to inspect, and soon came upon Lobo's trail running from trap to trap. In the dust I could read the whole story of his doings that night. He had trotted along in the darkness, and although the traps were so carefully concealed, he had instantly detected the first one. Stopping the onward march of the pack, he had cautiously scratched around it until he had disclosed the trap, the chain, and the log, then left them wholly exposed to view with the trap still unsprung, and passing on he treated over a dozen traps in the same fashion. Very soon I noticed

31

that he stopped and turned aside as soon as
he detected suspicious signs on the trail and a
new plan to outwit him at once suggested itself.
I set the traps in the form of an H; that is,
with a row of traps on each side of the trail,
and one on the trail for the cross-bar of the H.
Before long, I had an opportunity to count another failure. Lobo came trotting along the trail,
and was fairly between the parallel lines before he detected the single trap in the trail, but
he stopped in time, and why or how he knew
enough I cannot tell, the Angel of the wild
things must have been with him, but without
turning an inch to the right or left, he slowly
and cautiously backed on his own tracks, putting each paw exactly in its old track until he
was off the dangerous ground. Then returning
at one side he scratched clods and stones with
his hind feet till he had sprung every trap. This
he did on many other occasions, and although
I varied my methods and redoubled my precau-
tions, he was never deceived, his sagacity seemed
never at fault, and he might have been pursuing
his career of rapine to-day, but for an unfortunate alliance that proved his ruin and added
his name to the long list of heroes who, unassail-

able when alone, have fallen through the indiscretion of a trusted ally.

III

Once or twice, I had found indications that everything was not quite right in the Currumpaw pack. There were signs of irregularity, I thought; for instance there was clearly the trail of a smaller wolf running ahead of the leader, at times, and this I could not understand until a cowboy made a remark which explained the matter.

" I saw them to-day, " he said, " and the wild one that breaks away is Blanca." Then the truth dawned upon me, and I added, " Now, I know that Blanca is a she-wolf, because were a he-wolf to act thus, Lobo would kill him at once."

This suggested a new plan. I killed a heifer, and set one or two rather obvious traps about the carcass. Then cutting off the head, which is considered useless offal, and quite beneath the notice of a wolf, I set it a little apart and around it placed two powerful steel traps proper-

ly deodorized and concealed with the utmost care. During my operations I kept my hands, boots, and implements smeared with fresh blood, and afterward sprinkled the ground with the same, as though it had flowed from the head ; and when the traps were buried in the dust I brushed the place over with the skin of a coyote, and with a foot of the same animal made a number of tracks over the traps. The head was so placed that there was a narrow passage between it and some tussocks, and in this passage I buried two of my best traps, fastening them to the head itself.

Wolves have a habit of approaching every carcass they get the wind of, in order to examine it, even when they have no intention of eating of it, and I hoped that this habit would bring the Currumpaw pack within reach of my latest stratagem. I did not doubt that Lobo would detect my handiwork about the meat, and prevent the pack approaching it, but I did build some hopes on the head, for it looked as though it had been thrown aside as useless.

Next morning, I sallied forth to inspect the traps, and there, oh, joy ! were the tracks of

Lobo

the pack, and the place where the beef-head and its traps had been was empty. A hasty study of the trail showed that Lobo had kept the pack from approaching the meat, but one, a small wolf, had evidently gone on to examine the head as it lay apart and had walked right into one of the traps.

We set out on the trail, and within a mile discovered that the hapless wolf was Blanca. Away she went, however, at a gallop, and although encumbered by the beef-head, which weighed over fifty pounds, she speedily distanced my companion who was on foot. But we overtook her when she reached the rocks, for the horns of the cow's head became caught and held her fast. She was the handsomest wolf I had ever seen. Her coat was in perfect condition and nearly white.

She turned to fight, and raising her voice in the rallying cry of her race, sent a long howl rolling over the cañon. From far away upon the mesa came a deep response, the cry of Old Lobo. That was her last call, for now we had closed in on her, and all her energy and breath were devoted to combat.

35

Then followed the inevitable tragedy, the idea of which I shrank from afterward more than at the time. We each threw a lasso over the neck of the doomed wolf, and strained our horses in opposite directions until the blood burst from her mouth, her eyes glazed, her limbs stiffened and then fell limp. Homeward then we rode, carrying the dead wolf, and exulting over this, the first death-blow we had been able to inflict on the Currumpaw pack.

At intervals during the tragedy, and afterward as we rode homeward, we heard the roar of Lobo as he wandered about on the distant mesas, where he seemed to be searching for Blanca. He had never really deserted her, but knowing that he could not save her, his deep-rooted dread of firearms had been too much for him when he saw us approaching. All that day we heard him wailing as he roamed in his quest, and I remarked at length to one of the boys, " Now, indeed, I truly know that Blanca was his mate."

As evening fell he seemed to be coming toward the home cañon, for his voice sounded continually nearer. There was an unmistakable

Lobo

note of sorrow in it now. It was no longer the loud, defiant howl, but a long, plaintive wail; " Blanca! Blanca!" he seemed to call. And as night came down, I noticed that he was not far from the place where we had overtaken her. At length he seemed to find the trail, and when he came to the spot where we had killed her, his heart-broken wailing was piteous to hear. It was sadder than I could possibly have believed. Even the stolid cowboys noticed it, and said they had " never heard a wolf carry on like that before." He seemed to know exactly what had taken place, for her blood had stained the place of her death.

Then he took up the trail of the horses and followed it to the ranch-house. Whether in hopes of finding her there, or in quest of revenge, I know not, but the latter was what he found, for he surprised our unfortunate watch-dog outside and tore him to little bits within fifty yards of the door. He evidently came alone this time, for I found but one trail next morning, and he had galloped about in a reckless manner that was very unusual with him. I had half expected this, and had set a number of additional traps about the pasture. Afterward I found that he had indeed fallen into one of these, but such was his strength, he had torn himself loose and cast it aside.

I believed that he would continue in the neighborhood until he found her body at least, so I concentrated all my energies on this one enterprise of catching him before he left the region, and while yet in this reckless mood. Then I realized what a mistake I had made in killing Blanca, for by using her as a decoy I might have secured him the next night.

I gathered in all the traps I could command, one hundred and thirty strong steel wolf-traps, and set them in fours in every trail that led into the cañon; each trap was separately fastened to a log, and each log was separately buried. In burying them, I carefully removed the sod and every particle of earth that was lifted we put in blankets, so that after the sod was replaced and all was finished the eye could detect no trace of human handiwork. When the traps were concealed I trailed the body of poor Blanca over each place, and made of it a drag that circled all about the ranch, and finally I took off one of her paws and made with it a line of tracks over each trap. Every precaution and device known to me I used, and retired at a late hour to await the result.

Once during the night I thought I heard Old Lobo, but was not sure of it. Next day I rode around, but darkness came on before I completed the circuit of the north cañon, and I had nothing to report. At supper one of the cowboys said, "There was a great row among the cattle in the north cañon this morning, maybe there is something in the traps there." It was afternoon of the next day before I got to the place referred to, and as I drew near a great grizzly form arose from the ground, vainly endeavoring to escape, and there revealed before me stood Lobo, King of the Currumpaw, firmly held in the traps. Poor old hero, he had never ceased to search for his darling, and when he found the trail her body had made he followed it recklessly, and so fell into the snare prepared for him. There he lay in the iron grasp of all four traps, perfectly helpless, and all around him were numerous tracks showing how the cattle had gathered about him to insult the fallen despot, without daring to approach within his reach. For two days and two nights he had lain there, and now was worn out with struggling. Yet, when I went near him, he rose up with bristling mane and raised his voice, and for the last time made the cañon reverberate with his deep bass roar, a call for help, the muster call of his band. But there was none to answer him, and, left alone in his extremity, he whirled about with all his strength and made a desperate effort to get at me. All in vain, each trap was a dead drag of over three hundred pounds, and in their relentless fourfold grasp, with great steel jaws on every foot, and the heavy logs and chains all entangled together, he was absolutely powerless. How his huge ivory tusks did grind on those cruel chains, and when I ventured to touch him with my rifle-barrel he left grooves on it which are there to this day. His eyes glared green with hate and fury, and his jaws snapped with a hollow ' chop,' as he vainly endeavored to reach me and my trembling horse. But he was worn out with hunger and struggling and loss of blood, and he soon sank exhausted to the ground.

Something like compunction came over me, as I prepared to deal out to him that which so many had suffered at his hands.

"Grand old outlaw, hero of a thousand lawless raids, in a few minutes you will be but a great load of carrion. It cannot be otherwise." Then I swung my lasso and sent it whistling over his head. But not so fast; he was yet far from being subdued, and, before the supple coils had fallen on his neck he seized the noose and, with one fierce chop, cut through its hard thick strands, and dropped it in two pieces at his feet.

Of course I had my rifle as a last resource, but I did not wish to spoil his royal hide, so I galloped back to the camp and returned with a cowboy and a fresh lasso. We threw to our victim a stick of wood which he seized in his teeth, and before he could relinquish it our lassoes whistled through the air and tightened on his neck.

Yet before the light had died from his fierce eyes, I cried, "Stay, we will not kill him; let us take him alive to the camp." He was so completely powerless now that it was easy to put a stout stick through his mouth, behind his tusks, and then lash his jaws with a heavy cord which was also fastened to the stick. The stick kept the cord in, and the cord kept the stick in so he was harmless. As soon as he felt his jaws were tied he made no further resistance, and uttered no sound, but looked calmly at us and seemed to say, " Well, you have got me at last, do as you please with me." And from that time he took no more notice of us.

We tied his feet securely, but he never groaned, nor growled, nor turned his head. Then with our united strength were just able to put him on my horse. His breath came evenly as though sleeping, and his eyes were bright and clear again, but did not rest on us. Afar on the great rolling mesas they were fixed, his passing kingdom, where his famous band was now scattered. And he gazed till the pony descended the pathway into the cañon, and the rocks cut off the view.

By travelling slowly we reached the ranch in safety, and after securing him with a collar and a strong chain, we staked him out in the pasture and removed the cords. Then for the first

time I could examine him closely, and proved
how unreliable is vulgar report when a living
hero or tyrant is concerned. He had *not* a
collar of gold about his neck, nor was there on
his shoulders an inverted cross to denote that
he had leagued himself with Satan. But I did
find on one haunch a great broad scar, that
tradition says was the fang-mark of Juno, the
leader of Tannerey's wolf-hounds — a mark
which she gave him the moment before he
stretched her lifeless on the sand of the cañon.

I set meat and water beside him, but he paid
no heed. He lay calmly on his breast, and
gazed with those steadfast yellow eyes away
past me down through the gateway of the cañon,
over the open plains—his plains—nor moved a
muscle when I touched him. When the sun
went down he was still gazing fixedly across the
prairie. I expected he would call up his band
when night came, and prepared for them, but
he had called once in his extremity, and none
had come; he would never call again.

A lion shorn of his strength, an eagle robbed
of his freedom, or a dove bereft of his mate, all
die, it is said, of a broken heart; and who will

43

aver that this grim bandit could bear the three-fold brunt, heart-whole? This only I know, that when the morning dawned, he was lying there still in his position of calm repose, but his spirit was gone—the old king-wolf was dead.

I took the chain from his neck, a cowboy helped me to carry him to the shed where lay the remains of Blanca, and as we laid him beside her, the cattle-man exclaimed: "There, you *would* come to her, now you are together again."

44

Silverspot
The Story of a Crow

Silverspot

The Story of a Crow

OW many of us have ever got to know a wild animal? I do not mean merely to meet with one once or twice, or to have one in a cage, but to really know it for a long time while it is wild, and to get an insight into its life and history. The trouble usually is to know one creature from his fellow. One fox or crow is so much like another that we cannot be sure that it really is the same next time we meet. But once in awhile there arises an animal who is stronger or wiser than his fellow, who becomes a great leader, who is, as we would say, a genius, and if he is bigger,

47

Silverspot

or has some mark by which men can know him, he soon becomes famous in his country, and shows us that the life of a wild animal may be far more interesting and exciting than that of many human beings.

Of this class were Courtant, the bob-tailed wolf that terrorized the whole city of Paris for about ten years in the beginning of the fourteenth century ; Clubfoot, the lame grizzly bear that left such a terrific record in the San Joaquin Valley of California ; Lobo, the king-wolf of New Mexico, that killed a cow every day for five years, and the Seonee panther that in less than two years killed nearly three hundred human beings—and such also was Silverspot, whose history, so far as I could learn it, I shall now briefly tell.

Silverspot was simply a wise old crow ; his name was given because of the silvery white spot that was like a nickel, stuck on his right side, between the eye and the bill, and it was owing to this spot that I was able to know him from the other crows, and put together the parts of his history that came to my knowledge.

Silverspot

Crows are, as you must know, our most intelligent birds—'Wise as an old crow' did not become a saying without good reason. Crows know the value of organization, and are as well drilled as soldiers—very much better than some soldiers, in fact, for crows are always on duty, always at war, and always dependent on each other for life and safety. Their leaders not only are the oldest and wisest of the band, but also the strongest and bravest, for they must be ready at any time with sheer force to put down an upstart or a rebel. The rank and file are the youngsters and the crows without special gifts.

Old Silverspot was the leader of a large band of crows that made their headquarters near Toronto, Canada, in Castle Frank, which is a pine-clad hill on the northeast edge of the city. This band numbered about two hundred, and for reasons that I never understood did not increase. In mild winters they stayed along the Niagara River; in cold winters they went much farther south. But each year in the last week of February Old Silverspot would muster his followers and boldly cross the forty miles of

49

open water that lies between Toronto and Niagara ; not, however, in a straight line would he go, but always in a curve to the west, whereby he kept in sight of the familiar landmark of Dundas Mountain, until the pine-clad hill itself came in view. Each year he came with his troop, and for about six weeks took up his abode on the hill. Each morning thereafter the crows set out in three bands to forage. One band went southeast to Ashbridge's Bay. One went north up the Don, and one, the largest, went northwestward up the ravine. The last Silverspot led in person. Who led the others I never found out.

On calm mornings they flew high and straight away. But when it was windy the band flew low, and followed the ravine for shelter. My windows overlooked the ravine, and it was thus that in 1885 I first noticed this old crow. I was a new-comer in the neighborhood, but an old resident said to me then "that there old crow has been a-flying up and down this ravine for more than twenty years." My chances to watch were in the ravine, and Silverspot doggedly clinging to the old route, though now it

50

was edged with houses and spanned by bridges, became a very familiar acquaintance. Twice each day in March and part of April, then again in the late summer and the fall, he passed and repassed, and gave me chances to see his movements, and hear his orders to his bands, and so, little by little, opened my eyes to the fact that the crows, though a little people, are of great wit, a race of birds with a language and a social system that is wonderfully human in many of its chief points, and in some is better carried out than our own.

One windy day I stood on the high bridge across the ravine, as the old crow, heading his long, straggling troop, came flying down homeward. Half a mile away I could hear the contented *'All's well, come right along!'* as we

No. 1.

Caw   Caw

should say, or as he put it, and as also his lieutenant echoed it at the rear of the band. They were flying very low to be out of the wind, and

51

would have to rise a little to clear the bridge
on which I was. Silverspot saw me standing
there, and as I was closely watching him he
didn't like it. He checked his flight and called
out, ' *Be on your guard*,' or

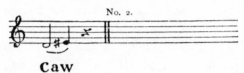

Caw

and rose much higher in the air. Then seeing
that I was not armed he flew over my head
about twenty feet, and his followers in turn did
the same, dipping again to the old level when
past the bridge.

Next day I was at the same place, and as
the crows came near I raised my walking stick
and pointed it at them. The old fellow at once
cried out ' *Danger*,' and rose fifty feet higher

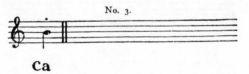

Ca

than before. Seeing that it was not a gun, he
ventured to fly over. But on the third day I

took with me a gun, and at once he cried out, '*Great danger—a gun.*' His lieutenant re-

ca ca ca ca Caw

peated the cry, and every crow in the troop began to tower and scatter from the rest, till they were far above gun shot, and so passed safely over, coming down again to the shelter of the valley when well beyond reach. Another time, as the long, straggling troop came down the valley, a red-tailed hawk alighted on a tree close by their intended route. The leader cried out, '*Hawk, hawk,*' and stayed

Caw   Caw

his flight, as did each crow on nearing him, until all were massed in a solid body. Then, no longer fearing the hawk, they passed on. But a quarter of a mile farther on a man with a gun appeared below, and the cry, '*Great*

53

danger—a gun, a gun; scatter for your lives,'
at once caused them to scatter widely and tower

ca ca ca ca   Caw

till far beyond range. Many others of his
words of command I learned in the course of
my long acquaintance, and found that sometimes
a very little difference in the sound makes a
very great difference in meaning.   Thus while
No. 5 means hawk, or any large, dangerous
bird, this means *'wheel around,'* evidently a

Caw   Caw   ca ca ca ca

combination of No. 5, whose root idea is danger, and of No. 4, whose root idea is retreat, and
this again is a mere *'good day,'* to a far away

Caw   Caw

comrade. This is usually addressed to the ranks and means ' *attention.* '

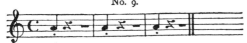

Early in April there began to be great doings among the crows. Some new cause of excitement seemed to have come on them. They spent half the day among the pines, instead of foraging from dawn till dark. Pairs and trios might be seen chasing each other, and from time to time they showed off in various feats of flight. A favorite sport was to dart down suddenly from a great height toward some perching crow, and just before touching it to turn at a hairbreadth and rebound in the air so fast that the wings of the swooper whirred with a sound like distant thunder. Sometimes one crow would lower his head, raise every feather, and coming close to another would gurgle out a long note like

No. 10.

C – r – r – r – a – w

55

What did it all mean ? I soon learned. They were making love and pairing off. The males were showing off their wing powers and their voices to the lady crows. And they must have been highly appreciated, for by the middle of April all had mated and had scattered over the country for their honeymoon, leaving the sombre old pines of Castle Frank deserted and silent.

II

The Sugar Loaf hill stands alone in the Don Valley. It is still covered with woods that join with those of Castle Frank, a quarter of a mile off. In the woods, between the two hills, is a pine-tree in whose top is a deserted hawk's nest. Every Toronto school-boy knows the nest, and, excepting that I had once shot a black squirrel on its edge, no one had ever seen a sign of life about it. There it was year after year, ragged and old, and falling to pieces. Yet, strange to tell, in all that time it never did drop to pieces, like other old nests.

One morning in May I was out at gray dawn, and stealing gently through the woods, whose

Silverspot

dead leaves were so wet that no rustle was made,
I chanced to pass under the old nest, and was
surprised to see a black tail sticking over the
edge.   I struck the tree a smart blow, off flew
a crow, and the secret was out.   I had long
suspected that a pair of crows nested each year
about the pines, but now I realized that it was
Silverspot and his wife.   The old nest was
theirs, and they were too wise to give it an air
of spring-cleaning and housekeeping each year.
Here they had nested for long, though guns in
the hands of men and boys hungry to shoot
crows were carried under their home every day.
I never surprised the old fellow again, though I
several times saw him through my telescope.

One day while watching I saw a crow crossing
the Don Valley with something white in his
beak.   He flew to the mouth of the Rosedale
Brook, then took a short flight to the Beaver
Elm.   There he dropped the white object, and
looking about gave me a chance to recognize
my old friend Silverspot.   After a minute he
picked up the white thing—a shell—and walked
over past the spring, and here, among the docks
and the skunk-cabbages, he unearthed a pile of

57

shells and other white, shiny things. He spread them out in the sun, turned them over, lifted them one by one in his beak, dropped them, nestled on them as though they were eggs, toyed with them and gloated over them like a miser. This was his hobby, his weakness. He could not have explained *why* he enjoyed them, any more than a boy can explain why he collects postage-stamps, or a girl why she prefers pearls to rubies ; but his pleasure in them was very real, and after half an hour he covered them all, in-cluding the new one, with earth and leaves, and flew off. I went at once to the spot and examined the hoard ; there was about a hatful in all, chiefly white pebbles, clam-shells, and some bits of tin, but there was also the handle of a china cup, which must have been the gem of the collection. That was the last time I saw them. Silverspot knew that I had found his treasures, and he removed them at once ; where I never knew.

During the space that I watched him so closely he had many little adventures and escapes. He was once severely handled by a sparrowhawk, and often he was chased and

worried by kingbirds. Not that these did him much harm, but they were such noisy pests that he avoided their company as quickly as possible, just as a grown man avoids a conflict with a noisy and impudent small boy. He had some cruel tricks, too. He had a way of going the round of the small birds' nests each morning to eat the new laid eggs, as regularly as a doctor visiting his patients. But we must not judge him for that, as it is just what we ourselves do to the hens in the barnyard.

His quickness of wit was often shown. One day I saw him flying down the ravine with a large piece of bread in his bill. The stream below him was at this time being bricked over as a sewer. There was one part of two hundred yards quite finished, and, as he flew over the open water just above this, the bread fell from his bill, and was swept by the current out of sight into the tunnel. He flew down and peered vainly into the dark cavern, then, acting upon a happy thought, he flew to the downstream end of the tunnel, and awaiting the reappearance of the floating bread, as it was swept

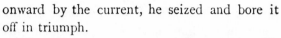

onward by the current, he seized and bore it off in triumph.

Silverspot was a crow of the world. He was truly a successful crow. He lived in a region that, though full of dangers, abounded with food. In the old, unrepaired nest he raised a brood each year with his wife, whom, by the way, I never could distinguish,. and when the crows again gathered together he was their acknowledged chief.

The reassembling takes place about the end of June—the young crows with their bob-tails, soft wings, and falsetto voices are brought by their parents, whom they nearly equal in size, and introduced to society at the old pine woods, a woods that is at once their fortress and college. Here they find security in numbers and in lofty yet sheltered perches, and here they begin their schooling and are taught all the secrets of success in crow life, and in crow life the least failure does not simply mean begin again. It means *death*.

The first week or two after their arrival is spent by the young ones in getting acquainted, for each crow must know personally all the

Silverspot

others in the band. Their parents meanwhile have time to rest a little after the work of raising them, for now the youngsters are able to feed themselves and roost on a branch in a row, just like big folks.

In a week or two the moulting season comes. At this time the old crows are usually irritable and nervous, but it does not stop them from beginning to drill the youngsters, who, of course, do not much enjoy the punishment and nagging they get so soon after they have been mamma's own darlings. But it is all for their good, as the old lady said when she skinned the eels, and old Silverspot is an excellent teacher. Sometimes he seems to make a speech to them. What he says I cannot guess, but, judging by the way they receive it, it must be extremely witty. Each morning there is a company drill, for the young ones naturally drop into two or three squads according to their age and strength. The rest of the day they forage with their parents.

When at length September comes we find a great change. The rabble of silly little crows have begun to learn sense. The delicate blue iris of their eyes, the sign of a fool-crow, has given place to the dark brown eye of the old stager. They know their drill now and have learned sentry duty. They have been taught guns and traps and taken a special course in wire-worms and greencorn. They know that a fat old farmer's wife is much less dangerous, though so much larger, than her fifteen-year-old son, and they can tell the boy from his sister.

They know that an umbrella is not a gun, and they can count up to six, which is fair for young crows, though Silverspot can go up nearly to thirty. They know the smell of gunpowder and the south side of a hemlock-tree, and begin to plume themselves upon being crows of the world. They always fold their wings three times after alighting, to be sure that it is neatly done. They know how to worry a fox into giving up half his dinner, and also that when the kingbird or the purple martin assails them they must dash into a bush, for it is as impossible to fight the little pests as it is for the fat apple-woman to catch the small boys who have raided her basket. All these things do the young crows know ; but they have taken

Silverspot

no lessons in egg-hunting yet, for it is not the season. They are unacquainted with clams, and have never tasted horses' eyes, or seen sprouted corn, and they don't know a thing about travel, the greatest educator of all. They did not think of that two months ago, and since then they have thought of it, but have learned to wait till their betters are ready.

September sees a great change in the old crows, too. Their moulting is over. They are now in full feather again and proud of their handsome coats. Their health is again good, and with it their tempers are improved. Even old Silverspot, the strict teacher, becomes quite jolly, and the youngsters, who have long ago learned to respect him, begin really to love him.

He has hammered away at drill, teaching them all the signals and words of command in use, and now it is a pleasure to see them in the early morning.

' *Company 1 !* ' the old chieftain would cry in crow, and Company 1 would answer with a great clamor.

' *Fly !* ' and himself leading them, they would all fly straight forward.

'*Mount!*' and straight upward they turned in a moment.

'*Bunch!*' and they all massed into a dense black flock.

'*Scatter!*' and they spread out like leaves before the wind.

'*Form line!*' and they strung out into the long line of ordinary flight.

'*Descend!*' and they all dropped nearly to the ground.

'*Forage!*' and they alighted and scattered about to feed, while two of the permanent sentries mounted duty—one on a tree to the right, the other on a mound to the far left. A minute or two later Silverspot would cry out, '*A man with a gun!*' The sentries repeated the cry and the company flew at once in open order as quickly as possible toward the trees. Once behind these, they formed line again in safety and returned to the home pines.

Sentry duty is not taken in turn by all the crows, but a certain number whose watchfulness has been often proved are the perpetual sentries, and are expected to watch and forage at the same time. Rather hard on them it seems to

64

Silverspot

us, but it works well and the crow organization is admitted by all birds to be the very best in existence.

Finally, each November sees the troop sail away southward to learn new modes of life, new landmarks and new kinds of food, under the guidance of the ever-wise Silverspot.

III

There is only one time when a crow is a fool, and that is at night. There is only one bird that terrifies the crow, and that is the owl. When, therefore, these come together it is a woful thing for the sable birds. The distant hoot of an owl after dark is enough to make them withdraw their heads from under their wings, and sit trembling and miserable till morning. In very cold weather the exposure of their faces thus has often resulted in a crow having one or both of his eyes frozen, so that blindness followed and therefore death. There are no hospitals for sick crows.

Silverspot

But with the morning their courage comes again, and arousing themselves they ransack the woods for a mile around till they find that owl, and if they do not kill him they at least worry him half to death and drive him twenty miles away.

In 1893 the crows had come as usual to Castle Frank. I was walking in these woods a few days afterward when I chanced upon the track of a rabbit that had been running at full speed over the snow and dodging about among the trees as though pursued. Strange to tell, I could see no track of the pursuer. I followed the trail and presently saw a drop of blood on the snow, and a little farther on found the partly devoured remains of a little brown bunny. What had killed him was a mystery until a careful search showed in the snow a great double-toed track and a beautifully pencilled brown feather. Then all was clear—*a horned owl.* Half an hour later, in passing again by the place, there, in a tree, within ten feet of the bones of his victim, was the fierce-eyed owl himself. The murderer still hung about the scene of his crime. For once circumstantial evidence had not lied.

Silverspot

At my approach he gave a guttural '*grrr-oo*' and flew off with low flagging flight to haunt the distant sombre woods.

Two days afterward, at dawn, there was a great uproar among the crows. I went out early to see, and found some black feathers drifting over the snow. I followed up the wind in the direction from which they came and soon saw the bloody remains of a crow and the great double-toed track which again told me that the murderer was the owl. All around were signs of the struggle, but the fell destroyer was too strong. The poor crow had been dragged from his perch at night, when the darkness had put him at a hopeless disadvantage.

I turned over the remains, and by chance unburied the head—then started with an exclamation of sorrow. Alas! It was the head of old Silverspot. His long life of usefulness to his tribe was over—slain at last by the owl that he had taught so many hundreds of young crows to beware of.

The old nest on the Sugar Loaf is abandoned now. The crows still come in spring-time to Castle Frank, but without their famous leader

67

their numbers are dwindling, and soon they will be seen no more about the old pine-grove in which they and their forefathers had lived and learned for ages.

Raggylug
The Story of a
Cottontail Rabbit

Raggylug

The Story of a Cottontail Rabbit

RAGGYLUG, or Rag, was the name of a young
cottontail rabbit. It was given him from his
torn and ragged ear, a life-mark that he got
in his first adventure. He lived with his mother
in Olifant's swamp, where I made their acquaintance and gathered, in a hundred different ways,
the little bits of proof and scraps of truth that at
length enabled me to write this history.

Those who do not know the animals well
may think I have humanized them, but those
who have lived so near them as to know somewhat of their ways and their minds will not
think so.

Truly rabbits have no speech as we understand it, but they have a way of conveying ideas
by a system of sounds, signs, scents, whisker-

touches, movements, and example that answers
the purpose of speech; and it must be remembered that though in telling this story I free-
ly translate from rabbit into English, *I repeat
nothing that they did not say.*

I

The rank swamp grass bent over and concealed the snug nest where Raggylug's mother
had hidden him.   She had partly covered him
with some of the bedding, and, as always, her
last warning was to 'lay low and say nothing,
whatever happens.'   Though tucked in bed,
he was wide awake and his bright eyes were

taking in that part of his little green world that was straight above. A bluejay and a red-squirrel, two notorious thieves, were loudly berating each other for stealing, and at one time Rag's home bush was the centre of their fight; a yellow warbler caught a blue butterfly but six inches from his nose, and a scarlet and black ladybug, serenely waving her knobbed feelers, took a long walk up one grassblade, down another, and across the nest and over Rag's face—and yet he never moved nor even winked.

After a while he heard a strange rustling of the leaves in the near thicket. It was an odd, continuous sound, and though it went this way and that way and came ever nearer, there was no patter of feet with it. Rag had lived his whole life in the Swamp (he was three weeks old) and yet had never heard anything like this. Of course his curiosity was greatly aroused. His mother had cautioned him to lay low, but that was understood to be in case of danger, and this strange sound without footfalls could not be anything to fear.

The low rasping went past close at hand, then to the right, then back, and seemed going away. Rag felt he knew what he was about; he wasn't a baby; it was his duty to learn what it was. He slowly raised his roly-poly body on his short fluffy legs, lifted his little round head above the covering of his nest and peeped out into the woods. The sound had ceased as soon as he moved. He saw nothing, so took one step forward to a clear view, and instantly found himself face to face with an enormous Black Serpent.

"Mammy," he screamed in mortal terror as the monster darted at him. With all the strength of his tiny limbs he tried to run. But in a flash the Snake had him by one ear and whipped around him with his coils to gloat over the helpless little baby bunny he had secured for dinner.

"Mam-my—Mam-my," gasped poor little Raggylug as the cruel monster began slowly choking him to death. Very soon the little one's cry would have ceased, but bounding through the woods straight as an arrow came Mammy. No longer a shy, helpless little Molly Cottontail, ready to fly from a shadow: the mother's love was strong in her. The cry of

74

her baby had filled her with the courage of a hero, and—hop, she went over that horrible reptile. Whack, she struck down at him with her sharp hind claws as she passed, giving him such a stinging blow that he squirmed with pain and hissed with anger.

"M-a-m-m-y," came feebly from the little one. And Mammy came leaping again and again and struck harder and fiercer until the loathsome reptile let go the little one's ear and tried to bite the old one as she leaped over. But all he got was a mouthful of wool each time, and Molly's fierce blows began to tell, as long bloody rips were torn in the Black Snake's scaly armor.

Things were now looking bad for the Snake; and bracing himself for the next charge, he lost his tight hold on Baby Bunny, who at once wriggled out of the coils and away into the underbrush, breathless and terribly frightened, but unhurt save that his left ear was much torn by the teeth of that dreadful Serpent.

Molly now had gained all she wanted. She had no notion of fighting for glory or revenge. Away she went into the woods and the little

one followed the shining beacon of her snow-
white tail until she led him to a safe corner of
the Swamp.

II

Old Olifant's Swamp was a rough, brambly
tract of second-growth woods, with a marshy
pond and a stream through the middle. A few
ragged remnants of the old forest still stood
in it and a few of the still older trunks were
lying about as dead logs in the brushwood.
The land about the pond was of that willow-
grown sedgy kind that cats and horses avoid,
but that cattle do not fear. The drier zones
were overgrown with briars and young trees.
The outermost belt of all, that next the fields,
was of thrifty, gummy - trunked young pines
whose living needles in air and dead ones on
earth offer so delicious an odor to the nostrils
of the passer-by, and so deadly a breath to
those seedlings that would compete with them
for the worthless waste they grow on.

All around for a long way were smooth
fields, and the only wild tracks that ever crossed

these fields were those of a thoroughly bad and unscrupulous fox that lived only too near.

The chief indwellers of the swamp were Molly and Rag. Their nearest neighbors were far away, and their nearest kin were dead. This was their home, and here they lived together, and here Rag received the training that made his success in life.

Molly was a good little mother and gave him a careful bringing up. The first thing he learned was ' to lay low and say nothing.' His adventure with the snake taught him the wisdom of this. Rag never forgot that lesson ; afterward he did as he was told, and it made the other things come more easily.

The second lesson he learned was ' freeze.' It grows out of the first, and Rag was taught it as soon as he could run.

' Freezing' is simply doing nothing, turning into a statue. As soon as he finds a foe near, no matter what he is doing, a well-trained Cottontail keeps just as he is and stops all movement, for the creatures of the woods are of the same color as the things in the woods and catch the eye only while moving. So when

enemies chance together, the one who first sees
the other can keep himself unseen by 'freezing' and thus have all the advantage of choosing the time for attack or escape. Only those
who live in the woods know the importance of
this ; every wild creature and every hunter
must learn it ; all learn to do it well, but not
one of them can beat Molly Cottontail in the
doing. Rag's mother taught him this trick
by example. When the white cotton cushion
that she always carried to sit on went bobbing
away through the woods, of course Rag ran his
hardest to keep up. But when Molly stopped
and 'froze,' the natural wish to copy made
him do the same.

But the best lesson of all that Rag learned
from his mother was the secret of the Brierbrush.
It is a very old secret now, and to make it
plain you must first hear why the Brierbrush
quarrelled with the beasts.

Raggylug

*Long ago the Roses used
to grow on bushes that had no thorns.
But the Squirrels and Mice used to
climb after them, the Cattle used to knock
them off with their horns, the Possum
would twitch them off with his long tail,
and the Deer, with his sharp hoofs, would
break them down. So the Brierbrush
armed itself with spikes to protect its roses
and declared eternal war on all creatures that
climbed trees, or had horns, or hoofs, or long
tails. This left the Brierbrush at peace with
none but Molly Cottontail, who could not climb,
was hornless, hoofless, and had scarcely any
tail at all.*

*In truth the Cottontail had never harmed a
Brierrose, and having now so many enemies
the Rose took the Rabbit into especial friend-
ship, and when dangers are threatening poor
Bunny he flies to the nearest Brierbrush, certain that it is ready with a million keen and
poisoned daggers to defend him.*

Raggylug

So the secret that Rag learned from his mother was, ' The Brierbush is your best friend.'

Much of the time that season was spent in learning the lay of the land, and the bramble and brier mazes. And Rag learned them so well that he could go all around the swamp by two different ways and never leave the friendly briers at any place for more than five hops.

It is not long since the foes of the Cotton-tails were disgusted to find that man had brought a new kind of bramble and planted it in long lines throughout the country. It was so strong that no creatures could break it down, and so sharp that the toughest skin was torn by it. Each year there was more of it and each year it became a more serious matter to the wild creatures. But Molly Cottontail had no fear of it. She was not brought up in the briers for nothing. Dogs and foxes, cattle and sheep, and even man himself might be torn by those fearful spikes: but Molly understands it and lives and thrives under it. And the further it spreads the more safe country there is for the Cottontail. And the name of this new and dreaded bramble is—*the barbed-wire fence.*

Raggylug

III

Molly had no other children to look after now, so Rag had all her care. He was unusually quick and bright as well as strong, and he had uncommonly good chances; so he got on remarkably well.

All the season she kept him busy learning the tricks of the trail, and what to eat and drink and what not to touch. Day by day she worked to train him; little by little she taught him, putting into his mind hundreds of ideas that her own life or early training had stored in hers, and so equipped him with the knowledge that makes life possible to their kind.

Close by her side in the clover-field or the thicket he would sit and copy her when she wobbled her nose 'to keep her smeller clear,' and pull the bite from her mouth or taste her lips to make sure he was getting the same kind of fodder. Still copying her, he learned to comb his ears with his claws and to dress his coat and to bite the burrs out of his vest and socks. He learned, too, that nothing but clear

dewdrops from the briers were fit for a rabbit
to drink, as water which has once touched the
earth must surely bear some taint. Thus he
began the study of woodcraft, the oldest of all
sciences.

As soon as Rag was big enough to go out
alone, his mother taught him the signal code.
Rabbits telegraph each other by thumping on
the ground with their hind feet. Along the
ground sound carries far; a thump that at six
feet from the earth is not heard at twenty yards
will, near the ground, be heard at least one
hundred yards. Rabbits have very keen hearing, and so might hear this same thump at two
hundred yards, and that would reach from end to
end of Olifant's Swamp. A single *thump* means
'look out' or 'freeze.' A slow *thump thump*
means 'come.' A fast *thump thump* means
'danger;' and a very fast *thump thump thump*
means 'run for dear life.'

At another time, when the weather was fine
and the bluejays were quarrelling among themselves, a sure sign that no dangerous foe was
about, Rag began a new study. Molly, by
flattening her ears, gave the sign to squat. Then

Raggylug

she ran far away in the thicket and gave the thumping signal for 'come.' Rag set out at a run to the place but could not find Molly. He thumped, but got no reply. Setting carefully about his search he found her foot-scent and following this strange guide, that the beasts all know so well and man does not know at all, he worked out the trail and found her where she was hidden. Thus he got his first lesson in trailing, and thus it was that the games of hide and seek they played became the schooling for the serious chase of which there was so much in his after life.

Before that first season of schooling was over he had learnt all the principal tricks by which a rabbit lives and in not a few problems showed himself a veritable genius.

He was an adept at 'tree,' 'dodge,' and 'squat,' he could play 'log-lump,' with 'wind' and ' baulk ' with ' back-track ' so well that he scarcely needed any other tricks. He had not yet tried it, but he knew just how to play ' barb-wire,' which is a new trick of the brilliant order ; he had made a special study of 'sand,' which burns up all scent, and he was deeply versed in 'change-off,' 'fence,' and 'double' as well as 'hole-up,' which is a trick requiring longer notice, and yet he never forgot that 'lay-low' is the beginning of all wisdom and 'brierbush' the only trick that is always safe.

He was taught the signs by which to know all his foes and then the way to baffle them. For hawks, owls, foxes, hounds, curs, minks, weasels, cats, skunks, coons, and men, each have a different plan of pursuit, and for each and all of these evils he was taught a remedy.

And for knowledge of the enemy's approach he learnt to depend first on himself and his mother, and then on the bluejay. "Never neglect the bluejay's warning," said Molly; "he is a mischief-maker, a marplot, and a thief all the time, but nothing escapes him. He wouldn't mind harming us, but he cannot, thanks to the briers, and his enemies are ours, so it is well to heed him. If the woodpecker cries a warning you can trust him, he is honest; but he is a fool beside the bluejay, and though the bluejay often tells lies for mischief you are safe to believe him when he brings ill news."

Raggylug

The barb-wire trick takes a deal of nerve and the best of legs. It was long before Rag ventured to play it, but as he came to his full powers it became one of his favorites.

"It's fine play for those who can do it," said Molly. " First you lead off your dog on a straightaway and warm him up a bit by nearly letting him catch you. Then keeping just one hop ahead, you lead him at a long slant full tilt into a breast-high barb-wire. I've seen many a dog and fox crippled, and one big hound killed outright this way. But I've also seen more than one rabbit lose his life in trying it."

Rag early learnt what some rabbits never learn at all, that 'hole-up' is not such a fine ruse as it seems; it may be the certain safety of a wise rabbit, but soon or late is a sure death-trap to a fool. A young rabbit always thinks of it first, an old rabbit never tries it till all others fail. It means escape from a man or dog, a fox or a bird of prey, but it means sudden death if the foe is a ferret, mink, skunk, or weasel.

There were but two ground-holes in the Swamp. One on the Sunning Bank, which was

a dry sheltered knoll in the South-end. It was open and sloping to the sun, and here on fine days the Cottontails took their sunbaths. They stretched out among the fragrant pine needles and winter-green in odd cat-like positions, and turned slowly over as though roasting and wishing all sides well done. And they blinked and panted, and squirmed as if in dreadful pain; yet this was one of the keenest enjoyments they knew.

Just over the brow of the knoll was a large pine stump. Its grotesque roots wriggled out above the yellow sand-bank like dragons, and under their protecting claws a sulky old woodchuck had digged a den long ago. He became more sour and ill-tempered as weeks went by, and one day waited to quarrel with Olifant's dog instead of going in so that Molly Cottontail was able to take possession of the den an hour later.

This, the pine-root hole, was afterward very coolly taken by a self-sufficient young skunk who with less valor might have enjoyed greater longevity, for he imagined that even man with a gun would fly from him. Instead of keeping

86

Raggylug

Molly from the den for good, therefore, his reign, like that of a certain Hebrew king, was over in seven days.

The other, the fern-hole, was in a fern thicket next the clover field. It was small and damp, and useless except as a last retreat. It also was the work of a woodchuck, a well-meaning friendly neighbor, but a hare-brained youngster whose skin in the form of a whip-lash was now developing higher horse-power in the Olifant working team.

"Simple justice," said the old man, "for that hide was raised on stolen feed that the team would a' turned into horse-power anyway."

The Cottontails were now sole owners of the holes, and did not go near them when they could help it, lest anything like a path should be made that might betray these last retreats to an enemy.

There was also the hollow hickory, which, though nearly fallen, was still green, and had the great advantage of being open at both ends. This had long been the residence of one Lotor, a solitary old coon whose ostensible calling was frog-hunting, and who, like the monks of old,

was supposed to abstain from all flesh food. But it was shrewdly suspected that he needed but a chance to indulge in a diet of rabbit. When at last one dark night he was killed while raiding Olifant's hen-house, Molly, so far from feeling a pang of regret, took possession of his cosy nest with a sense of unbounded relief.

IV

Bright August sunlight was flooding the Swamp in the morning. Everything seemed soaking in the warm radiance. A little brown swamp-sparrow was teetering on a long rush in the pond. Beneath him there were open spaces of dirty water that brought down a few scraps of the blue sky, and worked it and the yellow duckweed into an exquisite mosaic, with a little wrong-side picture of the bird in the middle. On the bank behind was a great vigorous growth of golden green skunk-cabbage, that cast dense shadow over the brown swamp tussocks.

The eyes of the swamp-sparrow were not trained to take in the color glories, but he saw what we might have missed; that two of the numberless leafy brown bumps under the broad cabbage-leaves were furry living things, with noses that never ceased to move up and down whatever else was still.

It was Molly and Rag. They were stretched under the skunk-cabbage, not because they liked its rank smell, but because the winged ticks could not stand it at all and so left them in peace.

Rabbits have no set time for lessons, they are always learning; but what the lesson is depends on the present stress, and that must arrive before it is known. They went to this place for a quiet rest, but had not been long there when suddenly a warning note from the ever-watchful bluejay caused Molly's nose and ears to go up and her tail to tighten to her back. Away across the Swamp was Olifant's big black and white dog, coming straight toward them.

" Now," said Molly, "squat while I go and keep that fool out of mischief." Away she went to meet him and she fearlessly dashed across the dog's path.

" Bow-ow-ow," he fairly yelled as he bounded after Molly, but she kept just beyond his reach and led him where the million daggers struck fast and deep, till his tender ears were scratched raw, and guided him at last plump into a hidden barbed-wire fence, where he got such a gashing that he went homeward howling with pain. After making a short double, a loop and a baulk in case the dog should come back, Molly returned to find that Rag in his eagerness was standing bolt upright and craning his neck to see the sport.

This disobedience made her so angry that she struck him with her hind foot and knocked him over in the mud.

One day as they fed on the near clover field a red-tailed hawk came swooping after them. Molly kicked up her hind legs to make fun of him and skipped into the briers along one of their old pathways, where of course the hawk could not follow. It was the main path from the Creekside Thicket to the Stove-pipe brush-pile. Several creepers had grown across it, and Molly, keeping one eye on the hawk, set to work and cut the creepers off. Rag watched her, than ran on ahead, and cut some more that

were across the path. "That's right," said
Molly, "always keep the runways clear, you
will need them often enough. Not wide, but
clear. Cut everything like a creeper across
them and some day you will find you have
cut a snare. "A what?" asked Rag, as he
scratched his right ear with his left hind foot.

"A snare is something that looks like a
creeper, but it doesn't grow and it's worse than
all the hawks in the world," said Molly, glancing at the now far-away red-tail, "for there it
hides night and day in the runway till the
chance to catch you comes."

"I don't believe it could catch me," said
Rag, with the pride of youth as he rose on his
heels to rub his chin and whiskers high up on a
smooth sapling. Rag did not know he was doing
this, but his mother saw and knew it was a sign,
like the changing of a boy's voice, that her little
one was no longer a baby but would soon be a
grown-up Cottontail.

Raggylug

V

There is magic in running water. Who does not know it and feel it? The railroad builder fearlessly throws his bank across the wide bog or lake, or the sea itself, but the tiniest rill of running water he treats with great respect, studies its wish and its way and gives it all it seems to ask. The thirst-parched traveller in the poisonous alkali deserts holds back in deadly fear from the sedgy ponds till he finds one down whose centre is a thin, clear line, and a faint flow, the sign of running, living water, and joyfully he drinks.

There is magic in running water, no evil spell can cross it. Tam O'Shanter proved its potency in time of sorest need. The wild-wood creature with its deadly foe following tireless on the trail scent, realizes its nearing doom and feels an awful spell. Its strength is spent, its every trick is tried in vain till the good Angel leads it to the water, the running, living water, and dashing in it follows the cooling stream, and then with force renewed takes to the woods again.

Raggylug

There is magic in running water. The hounds come to the very spot and halt and cast about ; and halt and cast in vain. Their spell is broken by the merry stream, and the wild thing lives its life.

And this was one of the great secrets that Raggylug learned from his mother—" after the Brierrose, the Water is your friend."

One hot, muggy night in August, Molly led Rag through the woods. The cotton-white cushion she wore under her tail twinkled ahead and was his guiding lantern, though it went out as soon as she stopped and sat on it. After a few runs and stops to listen, they came to the edge of the pond. The hylas in the trees above them were singing ' *sleep, sleep,*' and away out on a sunken log in the deep water, up to his chin in the cooling bath, a bloated bullfrog was singing the praises of a '*jug o' rum.*'

" Follow me still," said Molly, in rabbit, and ' flop ' she went into the pond and struck out for the sunken log in the middle. Rag flinched but plunged with a little ' ouch,' gasping and wobbling his nose very fast but still copying his mother. The same movements as on land sent him through the water, and thus he found he could swim. On he went till he reached the sunken log and scrambled up by his dripping mother on the high dry end, with a rushy screen around them and the Water that tells no tales. After this in warm black nights when that old fox from Springfield came prowling through the Swamp, Rag would note the place of the bullfrog's voice, for in case of direst need it might be a guide to safety. And thenceforth the words of the song that the bullfrog sang were, ' *Come, come, in danger come.*'

This was the latest study that Rag took up with his mother—it was really a post-graduate course, for many little rabbits never learn it at all.

VI

No wild animal dies of old age. Its life has soon or late a tragic end. It is only a question of how long it can hold out against its foes. But Rag's life was proof that once a rabbit passes out of his youth he is likely to outlive his prime and be killed only in the last third of life, the downhill third we call old age.

The Cottontails had enemies on every side. Their daily life was a series of escapes. For dogs, foxes, cats, skunks, coons, weasels, minks, snakes, hawks, owls, and men, and even insects were all plotting to kill them. They had hundreds of adventures, and at least once a day they had to fly for their lives and save themselves by their legs and wits.

More than once that hateful fox from Springfield drove them to taking refuge under the wreck of a barbed-wire hog-pen by the spring. But once there they could look calmly at him while he spiked his legs in vain attempts to reach them.

Once or twice Rag when hunted had played off the hound against a skunk that had seemed likely to be quite as dangerous as the dog.

Once he was caught alive by a hunter who had a hound and a ferret to help him. But Rag had the luck to escape next day, with a yet deeper distrust of ground holes. He was several times run into the water by the cat, and many times was chased by hawks and owls, but

95

for each kind of danger there was a safeguard. His mother taught him the principal dodges, and he improved on them and made many new ones as he grew older. And the older and wiser he grew the less he trusted to his legs, and the more to his wits for safety.

Ranger was the name of a young hound in the neighborhood. To train him his master used to put him on the trail of one of the Cottontails. It was nearly always Rag that they ran, for the young buck enjoyed the runs as much as they did, the spice of danger in them being just enough for zest. He would say:

"Oh, mother! here comes the dog again, I must have a run to-day."

"You are too bold, Raggy, my son!" she might reply. "I fear you will run once too often."

"But, mother, it is such glorious fun to tease that fool dog, and it's all good training. I'll thump if I am too hard pressed, then you can come and change off while I get my second wind."

On he would come, and Ranger would take the trail and follow till Rag got tired of it. Then

96

Raggylug

he either sent a thumping telegram for help, which brought Molly to take charge of the dog, or he got rid of the dog by some clever trick. A description of one of these shows how well Rag had learned the arts of the woods.

He knew that his scent lay best near the ground, and was strongest when he was warm.

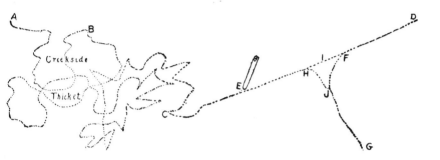

So if he could get off the ground, and be left in peace for half an hour to cool off, and for the trail to stale, he knew he would be safe. When, therefore, he tired of the chase, he made for the Creekside brier-patch, where he 'wound'— that is, zigzagged—till he left a course so crooked that the dog was sure to be greatly delayed in working it out. He then went straight to D in the woods, passing one hop to windward of the high log E. Stopping at D, he followed his back trail to F, here he leaped aside and ran toward G. Then, returning on his trail to J, he waited till the hound passed on his trail at I. Rag then got back on his old trail at H, and followed it to E, where, with a scent-baulk or great leap aside, he reached the high log, and running to its higher end, he sat like a bump.

Ranger lost much time in the bramble maze, and the scent was very poor when he got it straightened out, and came to D. Here he began to circle to pick it up, and after losing much time, struck the trail which ended suddenly at G. Again he was at fault, and had to circle to find the trail. Wider and wider the circles, until at last, he passed right under the log Rag was on. But a cold scent, on a cold day, does not go downward much. Rag never budged nor winked, and the hound passed.

Again the dog came round. This time he crossed the low part of the log, and stopped to smell it. 'Yes, clearly it was rabbity,' but it was a stale scent now ; still he mounted the log.

It was a trying moment for Rag, as the great

hound came sniff-sniffing along the log. But his
nerve did not forsake him; the wind was right;
he had his mind made up to bolt as soon as
Ranger came half way up. But he didn't come.
A yellow cur would have seen the rabbit sitting
there, but the hound did not, and the scent
seemed stale, so he leaped off the log, and Rag
had won.

VII

Rag had never seen any other rabbit than
his mother. Indeed he had scarcely thought
about there being any other. He was more
and more away from her now, and yet he never
felt lonely, for rabbits do not hanker for company. But one day in December, while he was
among the red dogwood brush, cutting a new
path to the great Creekside thicket, he saw all at
once against the sky over the Sunning Bank the
head and ears of a strange rabbit. The new-
comer had the air of a well-pleased discoverer
and soon came hopping Rag's way along one of
his paths into *his* Swamp. A new feeling rushed
over him, that boiling mixture of anger and
hatred called jealousy.

Raggylug

The stranger stopped at one of Rag's rubbing-trees—that is, a tree against which he used to stand on his heels and rub his chin as far up as he could reach. He thought he did this simply because he liked it; but all buck-rabbits do so, and several ends are served. It makes the tree rabbity, so that other rabbits know that this swamp already belongs to a rabbit family and is not open for settlement. It also lets the next one know by the scent if the last caller was an acquaintance, and the height from the ground of the rubbing-places shows how tall the rabbit is.

Now to his disgust Rag noticed that the newcomer was a head taller than himself, and a big, stout buck at that. This was a wholly new experience and filled Rag with a wholly new feeling. The spirit of murder entered his heart; he chewed very hard with nothing in his mouth, and hopping forward onto a smooth piece of hard ground he struck slowly:

'*Thump—thump—thump*,' which is a rabbit telegram for, ' Get out of my swamp, or fight.'

The new-comer made a big V with his ears, sat upright for a few seconds, then, dropping on his fore-feet, sent along the ground a louder, stronger, ' *Thump—thump—thump.*'

And so war was declared.

They came together by short runs side-wise, each one trying to get the wind of the other and watching for a chance advantage. The stranger was a big, heavy buck with plenty of muscle, but one or two trifles such as treading on a turnover and failing to close when Rag was on low ground showed that he had not much cunning and counted on winning his battles by his weight. On he came at last and Rag met him like a little fury. As they came together they leaped up and struck out with their hind feet. *Thud, thud* they came, and down went poor little Rag. In a moment the stranger was on him with his teeth and Rag was bitten, and lost several tufts of hair before he could get up. But he was swift of foot and got out of reach. Again he charged and again he was knocked down and bitten severely. He was no match for his foe, and it soon became a question of saving his own life.

Hurt as he was he sprang away, with the stranger in full chase, and bound to kill him as well as to oust him from the Swamp where he was born. Rag's legs were good and so was his wind. The stranger was big and so heavy that he soon gave up the chase, and it was well for poor Rag that he did, for he was getting stiff from his wounds as well as tired. From that day began a reign of terror for Rag. His training had been against owls, dogs, weasels, men, and so on, but what to do when chased by another rabbit, he did not know. All he knew was to lay low till he was found, then run.

Poor little Molly was completely terrorized; she could not help Rag and sought only to hide. But the big buck soon found her out. She tried to run from him, but she was not now so swift as Rag. The stranger made no attempt to kill her, but he made love to her, and because she hated him and tried to get away, he treated her shamefully. Day after day he worried her by following her about, and often, furious at her lasting hatred, he would knock her down and tear out mouthfuls of her soft fur till his rage cooled somewhat, when he would let her go for a while. But his fixed

purpose was to kill Rag, whose escape seemed
hopeless. There was no other swamp he could
go to, and whenever he took a nap now he
had to be ready at any moment to dash for his
life. A dozen times a day the big stranger came
creeping up to where he slept, but each time
the watchful Rag awoke in time to escape. To
escape yet not to escape. He saved his life indeed, but oh! what a miserable life it had become. How maddening to be thus helpless,
to see his little mother daily beaten and torn,
as well as to see all his favorite feeding-grounds,
the cosy nooks, and the pathways he had made
with so much labor, forced from him by this
hateful brute. Unhappy Rag realized that to
the victor belong the spoils, and he hated him
more than ever he did fox or ferret.

How was it to end? He was wearing out
with running and watching and bad food, and
little Molly's strength and spirit were breaking
down under the long persecution. The stranger
was ready to go to all lengths to destroy poor
Rag, and at last stooped to the worst crime
known among rabbits. However much they
may hate each other, all good rabbits forget

their feuds when their common enemy appears.
Yet one day when a great goshawk came swooping over the Swamp, the stranger, keeping well
under cover himself, tried again and again to
drive Rag into the open.

Once or twice the hawk nearly had him, but
still the briers saved him, and it was only when
the big buck himself came near being caught
that he gave it up. And again Rag escaped,
but was no better off. He made up his
mind to leave, with his mother, if possible, next
night and go into the world in quest of some
new home when he heard old Thunder, the
hound, sniffing and searching about the out-
skirts of the swamp, and he resolved on playing
a desperate game. He deliberately crossed the
hound's view, and the chase that then began was
fast and furious. Thrice around the Swamp
they went till Rag had made sure that his
mother was hidden safely and that his hated
foe was in his usual nest. Then right into that
nest and plump over him he jumped, giving him
a rap with one hind foot as he passed over his
head.

" You miserable fool, I kill you yet," cried

the stranger, and up he jumped only to find himself between Rag and the dog and heir to all the peril of the chase.

On came the hound baying hotly on the straight-away scent. The buck's weight and size were great advantages in a rabbit fight, but now they were fatal. He did not know many tricks. Just the simple ones like 'double,' 'wind,' and 'hole-up,' that every baby Bunny knows. But the chase was too close for doubling and winding, and he didn't know where the holes were.

It was a straight race. The brier-rose, kind to all rabbits alike, did its best, but it was no use. The baying of the hound was fast and steady. The crashing of the brush and the yelping of the hound each time the briers tore his tender ears were borne to the two rabbits where they crouched in hiding. But suddenly these sounds stopped, there was a scuffle, then loud and terrible screaming.

Rag knew what it meant and it sent a shiver through him, but he soon forgot that when all was over and rejoiced to be once more the master of the dear old Swamp.

VIII

Old Olifant had doubtless a right to burn all those brush-piles in the east and south of the Swamp and to clear up the wreck of the old barbed-wire hog-pen just below the spring. But it was none the less hard on Rag and his mother. The first were their various residences and outposts, and the second their grand fastness and safe retreat.

They had so long held the Swamp and felt it to be their very own in every part and suburb, —including Olifant's grounds and buildings— that they would have resented the appearance of another rabbit even about the adjoining barnyard.

Their claim, that of long, successful occupancy, was exactly the same as that by which most nations hold their land, and it would be hard to find a better right.

During the time of the January thaw the Olifants had cut the rest of the large wood about the pond and curtailed the Cottontails' domain on all sides. But they still clung to the dwindling Swamp, for it was their home and

they were loath to move to foreign parts.
Their life of daily perils went on, but they were
still fleet of foot, long of wind, and bright of
wit. Of late they had been somewhat troubled
by a mink that had wandered up-stream to their
quiet nook. A little judicious guidance had
transferred the uncomfortable visitor to Olifant's hen-house. But they were not yet quite
sure that he had been properly looked after. So
for the present they gave up using the ground-
holes, which were, of course, dangerous blind-
alleys, and stuck closer than ever to the briers
and the brush-piles that were left.

That first snow had quite gone and the
weather was bright and warm until now. Molly,
feeling a touch of rheumatism, was somewhere
in the lower thicket seeking a teaberry tonic.
Rag was sitting in the weak sunlight on a bank
in the east side. The smoke from the familiar gable chimney of Olifant's house came
fitfully drifting a pale blue haze through the
underwoods and showing as a dull brown
against the brightness of the sky. The sun-gilt
gable was cut off midway by the banks of brierbrush, that purple in shadow shone like rods of

blazing crimson and gold in the light. Beyond the house the barn with its gable and roof, new gilt as the house, stood up like a Noah's ark.

The sounds that came from it, and yet more the delicious smell that mingled with the smoke, told Rag that the animals were being fed cabbage in the yard. Rag's mouth watered at the idea of the feast. He blinked and blinked as he snuffed its odorous promises, for he loved cabbage dearly. But then he had been to the barnyard the night before after a few paltry clover-tops, and no wise rabbit would go two nights running to the same place.

Therefore he did the wise thing. He moved across where he could not smell the cabbage and made his supper of a bundle of hay that had been blown from the stack. Later, when about to settle for the night, he was joined by Molly, who had taken her teaberry and then eaten her frugal meal of sweet birch near the Sunning Bank.

Meanwhile the sun had gone about his business elsewhere, taking all his gold and glory with him. Off in the east a big black shutter came pushing up and rising higher and higher;

it spread over the whole sky, shut out all light
and left the world a very gloomy place indeed.
Then another mischief-maker, the wind, taking
advantage of the sun's absence, came on the scene
and set about brewing trouble. The weather
turned colder and colder ; it seemed worse than
when the ground had been covered with snow.

"Isn't this terribly cold ? How I wish we
had our stove-pipe brush-pile," said Rag.

"A good night for the pine-root hole," replied Molly, "but we have not yet seen the
pelt of that mink on the end of the barn, and
it is not safe till we do."

The hollow hickory was gone—in fact at this
very moment its trunk, lying in the wood-yard,
was harboring the mink they feared. So the
Cottontails hopped to the south side of the pond
and, choosing a brush-pile, they crept under and
snuggled down for the night, facing the wind
but with their noses in different directions so as
to go out different ways in case of alarm. The
wind blew harder and colder as the hours went
by, and about midnight a fine icy snow came
ticking down on the dead leaves and hissing
through the brush heap. It might seem a poor

night for hunting, but that old fox from Springfield was out. He came pointing up the wind
in the shelter of the Swamp and chanced in the
lee of the brush-pile, where he scented the
sleeping Cottontails. He halted for a moment,
then came stealthily sneaking up toward the
brush under which his nose told him the rabbits
were crouching. The noise of the wind and
the sleet enabled him to come quite close before Molly heard the faint crunch of a dry
leaf under his paw. She touched Rag's whiskers, and both were fully awake just as the fox
sprang on them; but they always slept with their
legs ready for a jump. Molly darted out into
the blinding storm. The fox missed his spring
but followed like a racer, while Rag dashed off
to one side.

There was only one road for Molly; that was
straight up the wind, and bounding for her
life she gained a little over the unfrozen mud
that would not carry the fox, till she reached
the margin of the pond. No chance to turn
now, on she must go.

Splash! splash! through the weeds she went,
then plunge into the deep water.

Raggylug

And plunge went the fox close behind. But it was too much for Reynard on such a night. He turned back, and Molly, seeing only one course, struggled through the reeds into the deep water and struck out for the other shore. But there was a strong headwind. The little waves, icy cold, broke over her head as she swam, and the water was full of snow that blocked her way like soft ice, or floating mud. The dark line of the other shore seemed far, far away, with perhaps the fox waiting for her there.

But she laid her ears flat to be out of the gale, and bravely put forth all her strength with wind and tide against her. After a long, weary swim in the cold water, she had nearly reached the farther reeds when a great mass of floating snow barred her road; then the wind on the bank made strange, fox-like sounds that robbed her of all force, and she was drifted far backward before she could get free from the floating bar.

Again she struck out, but slowly—oh so slowly now. And when at last she reached the lee of the tall reeds, her limbs were numbed, her strength spent, her brave little heart was sinking, and she cared no more whether the fox were there or not. Through the reeds she did indeed pass, but once in the weeds her course wavered and slowed, her feeble strokes no longer sent her landward, the ice forming around her, stopped her altogether. In a little while the cold, weak limbs ceased to move, the furry nose-tip of the little mother Cottontail wobbled no more, and the soft brown eyes were closed in death.

But there was no fox waiting to tear her with ravenous jaws. Rag had escaped the first onset of the foe, and as soon as he regained his wits he came running back to change-off and so help his mother. He met the old fox going round the pond to meet Molly and led him far and away, then dismissed him with a barbed-wire gash on his head, and came to the bank and sought about and trailed and thumped, but all his searching was in vain; he could not find his little mother. He never saw her again, and he never knew whither she went, for she slept her never-waking sleep in the ice-arms of her friend the Water that tells no tales.

Raggylug

Poor little Molly Cottontail! She was a true heroine, yet only one of unnumbered millions that without a thought of heroism have lived and done their best in their little world, and died. She fought a good fight in the battle of life. She was good stuff; the stuff that never dies. For flesh of her flesh and brain of her brain was Rag. She lives in him, and through him transmits a finer fibre to her race.

And Rag still lives in the Swamp. Old Olifant died that winter, and the unthrifty sons ceased to clear the Swamp or mend the wire fences. Within a single year it was a wilder place than ever; fresh trees and brambles grew, and falling wires made many Cottontail castles and last retreats that dogs and foxes dared not storm. And there to this day lives Rag. He is a big strong buck now and fears no rivals. He has a large family of his own, and a pretty brown wife that he got I know not where. There, no doubt, he and his children's children will flourish for many years to come, and there you may see them any sunny evening if you have learnt their signal code, and choosing a good spot on the ground, know just how and when to thump it.

Bingo
The Story of
My Dog

Bingo

"Ye Franckelyn's dogge leaped over a style,
And yey yclept him lyttel Bingo,
B = I = N = G = O ,
And yey yclept him lyttel Bingo.

Ye Franckelyn's wyfe brewed nutte=brown ayle,
And he yclept ytte rare goode Stingo,
S = T = I = N = G = O ,
And he yclept ytte rare goode Stingo.

Now ys not this a prettye rhyme,
I thynke ytte ys bye Jingo,
J = I = N = G = O ,
I thynke ytte ys bye Jingo."

Bingo

The Story of My Dog

I

T was early in November, 1882, and the Manitoba winter had just set in. I was tilting back in my chair for a few lazy moments after breakfast idly alternating my gaze from the one window-pane of our shanty, through which was framed a bit of the prairie and the end of our cowshed, to the old rhyme of the 'Franckelyn's dogge' pinned on the logs near by. But the dreamy mixture of rhyme and view was quickly dispelled by the sight of a large gray animal dashing across the prairie into the cowshed, with a smaller black and white animal in hot pursuit.

117

" A wolf," I exclaimed, and seizing a rifle
dashed out to help the dog. But before I
could get there they had left the stable, and
after a short run over the snow the wolf again
turned at bay, and the dog, our neighbor's
collie, circled about watching his chance to
snap.

I fired a couple of long shots, which had
the effect only of setting them off again over
the prairie. After another run this matchless
dog closed and seized the wolf by the haunch,
but again retreated to avoid the fierce return
chop. Then there was another stand at bay,
and again a race over the snow. Every few
hundred yards this scene was repeated. The
dog managing so that each fresh rush should be
toward the settlement, while the wolf vainly
tried to break back toward the dark belt of
trees in the east. At last after a mile of this
fighting and running I overtook them, and the
dog, seeing that he now had good backing,
closed in for the finish.

After a few seconds the whirl of struggling
animals resolved itself into a wolf, on his back,
with a bleeding collie gripping his throat, and

it was now easy for me to step up and end the fight by putting a ball through the wolf's head.

Then, when this dog of marvellous wind saw that his foe was dead, he gave him no second glance, but set out at a lope for a farm four miles across the snow where he had left his master when first the wolf was started. He was a wonderful dog, and even if I had not come he undoubtedly would have killed the wolf alone, as I learned he had already done with others of the kind, in spite of the fact that the wolf, though of the smaller or prairie race, was much larger than himself.

I was filled with admiration for the dog's prowess and at once sought to buy him at any price. The scornful reply of his owner was, "Why don't you try to buy one of the children?"

Since Frank was not in the market I was obliged to content myself with the next best thing, one of his alleged progeny. That is, a son of his wife. This probable offspring of an illustrious sire was a roly-poly ball of black fur that looked more like a long-tailed bear-cub than a puppy. But he had some tan markings like

those on Frank's coat, that were, I hoped, guar-
antees of future greatness, and also a very char-
acteristic ring of white that he always wore on
his muzzle.

Having got possession of his person, the next
thing was to find him a name. Surely this
puzzle was already solved. The rhyme of the
' Franckelyn's dogge ' was inbuilt with the foundation of our acquaintance, so with adequate
pomp we ' yclept him little Bingo.'

II

The rest of that winter Bingo spent in our
shanty, living the life of a lubberly, fat, well-
meaning, ill-doing puppy; gorging himself with
food and growing bigger and clumsier each day.
Even sad experience failed to teach him that he
must keep his nose out of the rat-trap. His most
friendly overtures to the cat were wholly mis-
understood and resulted only in an armed neu-
trality that, varied by occasional reigns of terror,
continued to the end ; which came when Bingo,
who early showed a mind of his own, got a

120

notion for sleeping at the barn and avoiding the shanty altogether.

When the spring came I set about his serious education. After much pains on my behalf and many pains on his, he learned to go at the word in quest of our old yellow cow, that pastured at will on the unfenced prairie.

Once he had learned his business, he became very fond of it and nothing pleased him more than an order to go and fetch the cow. Away he would dash, barking with pleasure and leaping high in the air that he might better scan the plain for his victim. In a short time he would return driving her at full gallop before him, and gave her no peace until, puffing and blowing, she was safely driven into the farthest corner of her stable.

Less energy on his part would have been more satisfactory, but we bore with him until he grew so fond of this semi-daily hunt that he began to bring ' old Dunne ' without being told. And at length not once or twice but a dozen times a day this energetic cowherd would sally forth on his own responsibility and drive the cow home to the stable.

Bingo

At last things came to such a pass that whenever he felt like taking a little exercise, or had a few minutes of spare time, or even happened to think of it, Bingo would sally forth at racing speed over the plain and a few minutes later return, driving the unhappy yellow cow at full gallop before him.

At first this did not seem very bad, as it kept the cow from straying too far; but soon it was seen that it hindered her feeding. She became thin and gave less milk; it seemed to weigh on her mind too, as she was always watching nervously for that hateful dog, and in the mornings would hang around the stable as though afraid to venture off and subject herself at once to an onset.

This was going too far. All attempts to make Bingo more moderate in his pleasure were failures, so he was compelled to give it up altogether. After this, though he dared not bring her home, he continued to show his interest by lying at her stable door while she was being milked.

As the summer came on the mosquitoes became a dreadful plague, and the consequent

vicious switching of Dunne's tail at milking-time even more annoying than the mosquitoes.

Fred, the brother who did the milking, was of an inventive as well as an impatient turn of mind, and he devised a simple plan to stop the switching. He fastened a brick to the cow's tail, then set blithely about his work assured of unusual comfort while the rest of us looked on in doubt.

Suddenly through the mist of mosquitoes came a dull whack and an outburst of 'language.' The cow went on placidly chewing till Fred got on his feet and furiously attacked her with the milking-stool. It was bad enough to be whacked on the ear with a brick by a stupid old cow, but the uproarious enjoyment and ridicule of the bystanders made it unendurable.

Bingo, hearing the uproar, and divining that he was needed, rushed in and attacked Dunne on the other side. Before the affair quieted down the milk was spilt, the pail and stool were broken, and the cow and the dog severely beaten.

Poor Bingo could not understand it at all. He had long ago learned to despise that cow,

and now in utter disgust he decided to for-sake even her stable door, and from that time he attached himself exclusively to the horses and their stable.

The cattle were mine, the horses were my brother's, and in transferring his allegiance from the cow-stable to the horse-stable Bingo seemed to give me up too, and anything like daily companionship ceased, and, yet, whenever any emergency arose Bingo turned to me and I to him, and both seemed to feel that the bond be-tween man and dog is one that lasts as long as life.

The only other occasion on which Bingo acted as cowherd was in the autumn of the same year at the annual Carberry Fair. Among the dazzling inducements to enter one's stock there was, in addition to a prospect of glory, a cash prize of 'two dollars,' for the 'best col-lie in training.'

Misled by a false friend, I entered Bingo, and early on the day fixed, the cow was driven to the prairie just outside of the village. When the time came she was pointed out to Bingo and the word given—'Go fetch the cow.' It was the intention, of course, tha⁺ he should bring her to me at the judge's stand.

But the animals knew better. They hadn't rehearsed all summer for nothing. When Dunne saw Bingo's careering form she knew that her only hope for safety was to get into her stable, and Bingo was equally sure that his sole mission in life was to quicken her pace in that direction. So off they raced over the prairie, like a wolf after a deer, and heading straight toward their home two miles away, they disappeared from view.

That was the last that judge or jury ever saw of dog or cow. The prize was awarded to the only other entry.

III

Bingo's loyalty to the horses was quite re-markable; by day he trotted beside them, and by night he slept at the stable door. Where the team went Bingo went, and nothing kept him away from them. This interesting assumption of ownership lent the greater significance to the following circumstance.

125

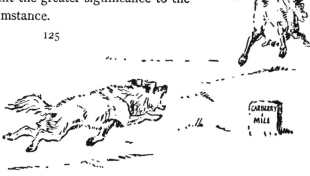

Bingo

I was not superstitious, and up to this time had had no faith in omens, but was now deeply impressed by a strange occurrence in which Bingo took a leading part. There were but two of us now living on the De Winton Farm. One morning my brother set out for Boggy Creek for a load of hay. It was a long day's journey there and back, and he made an early start. Strange to tell, Bingo for once in his life did not follow the team. My brother called to him, but still he stood at a safe distance, and eying the team askance, refused to stir. Suddenly he raised his nose in the air and gave vent to a long, melancholy howl. He watched the wagon out of sight, and even followed for a hundred yards or so, raising his voice from time to time in the most doleful howlings. All that day he stayed about the barn, the only time that he was willingly separated from the horses, and at intervals howled a very death dirge. I was alone, and the dog's behavior inspired me with an awful foreboding of calamity, that weighed upon me more and more as the hours passed away.

About six o'clock Bingo's howlings became

unbearable, so that for lack of a better thought I threw something at him, and ordered him away. But oh, the feeling of horror that filled me! Why did I let my brother go away alone? Should I ever again see him alive? I might have known from the dog's actions that something dreadful was about to happen.

At length the hour for his return arrived, and there was John on his load. I took charge of the horses, vastly relieved, and with an air of assumed unconcern, asked, "All right?"

"Right," was the laconic answer.

Who now can say that there is nothing in omens?

And yet, when long afterward, I told this to one skilled in the occult, he looked grave, and said, "Bingo always turned to you in a crisis?"

"Yes."

"Then do not smile. It was you that were in danger that day; he stayed and saved your life, though you never knew from what."

IV

Early in the spring I had begun Bingo's education. Very shortly afterward he began mine.

Midway on the two-mile stretch of prairie that lay between our shanty and the village of Carberry, was the corner-stake of the farm; it was a stout post in a low mound of earth, and was visible from afar.

I soon noticed that Bingo never passed without minutely examining this mysterious post. Next I learned that it was also visited by the prairie wolves as well as by all the dogs in the neighborhood, and at length, with the aid of a telescope, I made a number of observations that helped me to an understanding of the matter and enabled me to enter more fully into Bingo's private life.

The post was by common agreement a registry of the canine tribes. Their exquisite sense of smell enabled each individual to tell at once by the track and trace what other had recently been at the post. When the snow came much

Bingo

more was revealed. I then discovered that this post was but one of a system that covered the country ; that in short, the entire region was laid out in signal stations at convenient intervals. These were marked by any conspicuous post, stone, buffalo skull, or other object that chanced to be in the desired locality, and extensive observation showed that it was a very complete system for getting and giving the news.

Each dog or wolf makes a point of calling at those stations that are near his line of travel to learn who has recently been there, just as a man calls at his club on returning to town and looks up the register.

I have seen Bingo approach the post, sniff, examine the ground about, then growl, and with bristling mane and glowing eyes, scratch fiercely and contemptuously with his hind feet, finally walking off very stiffly, glancing back from time to time. All of which, being interpreted, said :

" *Grrrh! woof!* there's that dirty cur of McCarthy's. *Woof!* I'll 'tend to him to-night. *Woof! woof!*" On another occasion, after the preliminaries, he became keenly interested and studied a coyote's track that came and went, saying to himself, as I afterward learned :

"A coyote track coming from the north, smelling of dead cow. Indeed? Pollworth's old Brindle must be dead at last. This is worth looking into."

At other times he would wag his tail, trot about the vicinity and come again and again to make his own visit more evident, perhaps for the benefit of his brother Bill just back from Brandon! So that it was not by chance that one night Bill turned up at Bingo's home and was taken to the hills where a delicious dead horse afforded a chance to suitably celebrate the reunion.

At other times he would be suddenly aroused by the news, take up the trail, and race to the next station for later information.

Sometimes his inspection produced only an air of grave attention, as though he said to himself, "Dear me, who the deuce is this?" or "It seems to me I met that fellow at the Portage last summer."

One morning on approaching the post Bin-

130

"Who the deuce is this?"

Bingo

go's every hair stood on end, his tail dropped and quivered, and he gave proof that he was suddenly sick at the stomach, sure signs of terror. He showed no desire to follow up or know more of the matter, but returned to the house, and half an hour afterward his mane was still bristling and his expression one of hate or fear.

I studied the dreaded track and learned that in Bingo's language the half-terrified, deep-gurgled '*grrr-wff*' means '*timber wolf.*'

These were among the things that Bingo taught me. And in the after time when I might chance to see him arouse from his frosty nest by the stable door, and after stretching himself and shaking the snow from his shaggy coat, disappear into the gloom at a steady trot trot, trot, I used to think :

"Aha! old dog, I know where you are off to, and why you eschew the shelter of the shanty. Now I know why your nightly trips over the country are so well timed, and how you know just where to go for what you want, and when and how to seek it."

Bingo

V

In the autumn of 1884, the shanty at De
Winton farm was closed and Bingo changed
his home to the establishment, that is, to the
stable, not the house, of Gordon Wright, our
most intimate neighbor.

Since the winter of his puppyhood he had
declined to enter a house at any time excepting
during a thunder-storm. Of thunder and guns
he had a deep dread—no doubt the fear of the
first originated in the second, and that arose
from some unpleasant shot-gun experiences, the
cause of which will be seen. His nightly
couch was outside the stable, even during the
coldest weather, and it was easy to see that he
enjoyed to the full the complete nocturnal liberty
entailed. Bingo's midnight wanderings ex-
tended across the plains for miles. There was
plenty of proof of this. Some farmers at very
remote points sent word to old Gordon that if
he did not keep his dog home nights, they
would use the shotgun, and Bingo's terror of
firearms would indicate that the threats were

not idle. A man living as far away as Petrel, said he saw a large black wolf kill a coyote on the snow one winter evening, but afterward he changed his opinion and ' reckoned it must 'a' been Wright's dog.' Whenever the body of a winter-killed ox or horse was exposed, Bingo was sure to repair to it nightly, and driving away the prairie wolves, feast to repletion.

Sometimes the object of a night foray was merely to maul some distant neighbor's dog, and notwithstanding vengeful threats, there seemed no reason to fear that the Bingo breed would die out. One man even avowed that he had seen a prairie wolf accompanied by three young ones which resembled the mother, excepting that they were very large and black and had a ring of white around the muzzle.

True or not as that may be, I know that late in March, while we were out in the sleigh with Bingo trotting behind, a prairie wolf was started from a hollow. Away it went with Bingo in full chase, but the wolf did not greatly exert itself to escape, and within a short distance Bingo was close up, yet strange to tell, there was no grappling, no fight!

Bingo

Bingo trotted amiably alongside and licked the wolf's nose.

We were astounded, and shouted to urge Bingo on. Our shouting and approach several times started the wolf off at speed and Bingo again pursued until he had overtaken it, but his gentleness was too obvious.

"It is a she-wolf, he won't harm her," I exclaimed as the truth dawned on me. And Gordon said: "Well, I be darned."

So we called our unwilling dog and drove on.

For weeks after this we were annoyed by the depredations of a prairie wolf who killed our chickens, stole pieces of pork from the end of the house, and several times terrified the children by looking into the window of the shanty while the men were away.

Against this animal Bingo seemed to be no safeguard. At length the wolf, a female, was killed, and then Bingo plainly showed his hand by his lasting enmity toward Oliver, the man who did the deed.

Bingo

VI

It is wonderful and beautiful how a man and his dog will stick to one another, through thick and thin. Butler tells of an undivided Indian tribe, in the Far North which was all but exterminated by an internecine feud over a dog that belonged to one man and was killed by his neighbor; and among ourselves we have lawsuits, fights, and deadly feuds, all pointing the same old moral, 'Love me, love my dog.'

One of our neighbors had a very fine hound that he thought the best and dearest dog in the world. I loved him, so I loved his dog, and when one day poor Tan crawled home terribly mangled and died by the door, I joined my threats of vengeance with those of his master and thenceforth lost no opportunity of tracing the miscreant, both by offering rewards and by collecting scraps of evidence. At length it was clear that one of three men to the southward had had a hand in the cruel affair. The scent was warming up, and soon we should have been in a position to exact rigorous justice at least, from the wretch who had murdered poor old Tan.

Then something took place which at once changed my mind and led me to believe that the mangling of the old hound was not by any means an unpardonable crime, but indeed on second thoughts was rather commendable than otherwise.

Gordon Wright's farm lay to the south of us, and while there one day, Gordon, Jr., knowing that I was tracking the murderer, took me aside and looking about furtively, he whispered, in tragic tones :

" It was Bing done it."

And the matter dropped right there. For I confess that from that moment I did all in my power to baffle the justice I had previously striven so hard to further.

I had given Bingo away long before, but the feeling of ownership did not die; and of this indissoluble fellowship of dog and man he was soon to take part in another important illustration.

Old Gordon and Oliver were close neighbors and friends ; they joined in a contract to cut wood, and worked together harmoniously till late on in winter. Then Oliver's old horse died, and he, determining to profit as far as possible, dragged it out on the plain and laid poison baits for wolves around it. Alas, for poor Bingo! He would lead a wolfish life, though again and again it brought him into wolfish misfortunes.

He was as fond of dead horse as any of his wild kindred. That very night, with Wright's own dog Curley, he visited the carcass. It seemed as though Bing had busied himself chiefly keeping off the wolves, but Curley feasted immoderately. The tracks in the snow told the story of the banquet ; the interruption as the poison began to work, and of the dreadful spasms of pain during the erratic course back home where Curley, falling in convulsions at Gordon's feet, died in the greatest agony.

' Love me, love my dog,' no explanations or apology were acceptable ; it was useless to urge that it was accidental, the long-standing feud between Bingo and Oliver was now remembered as an important side-light. The wood-contract was thrown up, all friendly relations ceased, and to this day there is no county big enough to hold the rival factions which were called at once into existence and to arms by Curley's dying yell.

It was months before Bingo really recovered from the poison. We believed indeed that he never again would be the sturdy old-time Bingo. But when the spring came he began to gain strength, and bettering as the grass grew, he was within a few weeks once more in full health and vigor to be a pride to his friends and a nuisance to his neighbors.

VII

Changes took me far away from Manitoba, and on my return in 1886 Bingo was still a member of Wright's household. I thought he would have forgotten me after two years absence, but not so. One day early in the winter, after having been lost for forty-eight hours, he crawled home to Wright's with a wolf-trap and a heavy log fast to one foot, and the foot frozen to stony hardness. No one had been able to approach to help him, he was so savage, when I, the stranger now, stooped down and laid hold of the trap with one hand and his leg with the other. Instantly he seized my wrist in his teeth.

Without stirring I said, " Bing, don't you know me?"

He had not broken the skin and at once released his hold and offered no further resistance, although he whined a good deal during the removal of the trap. He still acknowledged me his master in spite of his change of residence and my long absence, and notwithstanding my surrender of ownership I still felt that he was my dog.

Bing was carried into the house much against his will and his frozen foot thawed out. During the rest of the winter he went lame and two of his toes eventually dropped off. But before the return of warm weather his health and strength were fully restored, and to a casual glance he bore no mark of his dreadful experience in the steel trap.

VIII

During that same winter I caught many wolves and foxes who did not have Bingo's good luck in escaping the traps, which I kept out right into the spring, for bounties are good even when fur is not.

Kennedy's Plain was always a good trapping ground because it was unfrequented by man and yet lay between the heavy woods and the settlement. I had been fortunate with the fur here, and late in April rode in on one of my regular rounds.

The wolf-traps are made of heavy steel and have two springs, each of one hundred pounds power. They are set in fours around a buried bait, and after being strongly fastened to concealed logs are carefully covered in cotton and in fine sand so as to be quite invisible.

A prairie wolf was caught in one of these. I killed him with a club and throwing him aside proceeded to reset the trap as I had done so many hundred times before. All was quickly done. I threw the trap-wrench over toward the pony, and seeing some fine sand near by, I reached out for a handful of it to add a good finish to the setting.

Oh, unlucky thought! Oh, mad heedlessness born of long immunity! That fine sand was *on the next wolf-trap* and in an instant I was a prisoner. Although not wounded, for the traps have no teeth, and my thick trapping gloves deadened the snap, I was firmly caught across the hand above the knuckles. Not greatly alarmed at this, I tried to reach the trap-wrench with my right foot. Stretching out at full length, face downward, I worked myself toward it, making my imprisoned arm as long and straight as possible. I could not see and reach at the same time, but counted on my toe telling me when I touched the little iron key to my fetters. My first effort was a failure; strain as I might at the chain my toe struck no metal. I swung slowly around my anchor, but still failed. Then a painfully taken observation showed I was much too far to the west. I set about working around, tapping blindly with my toe to discover the key. Thus wildly groping with my right foot I forgot

about the other till there was a sharp ' clank '
and the iron jaws of trap No. 3 closed tight on
my left foot.

The terrors of the situation did not, at
first, impress me, but I soon found that all my
struggles were in vain. I could not get free
from either trap or move the traps together,
and there I lay stretched out and firmly staked
to the ground.

What would become of me now ? There was
not much danger of freezing for the cold weather
was over, but Kennedy's Plain was never visited
excepting by the winter wood-cutters. No one
knew where I had gone, and unless I could man-
age to free myself there was no prospect ahead
but to be devoured by wolves, or else die of cold
and starvation.

As I lay there the red sun went down over the
spruce swamp west of the plain, and a shorelark
on a gopher mound a few yards off twittered his
evening song, just as one had done the night before at our shanty door, and though the numb
pains were creeping up my arm, and a deadly chill
possessed me, I noticed how long his little ear-
tufts were. Then my thoughts went to the com-

fortable supper-table at Wright's shanty, and I thought, now they are frying the pork for supper, or just sitting down. My pony still stood as I left him with his bridle on the ground patiently waiting to take me home. He did not understand the long delay, and when I called, he ceased nibbling the grass and looked at me in dumb, helpless inquiry. If he would only go home the empty saddle might tell the tale and bring help. But his very faithfulness kept him waiting hour after hour while I was perishing of cold and hunger.

Then I remembered how old Girou the trapper had been lost, and in the following spring his comrades found his skeleton held by the leg in a bear-trap. I wondered which part of my clothing would show my identity. Then a new thought came to me. This is how a wolf feels when he is trapped. Oh! what misery have I been responsible for! Now I'm to pay for it.

Night came slowly on. A prairie wolf howled, the pony pricked up his ears and walking nearer to me, stood with his head down. Then another prairie wolf howled and another, and I could make out that they were gathering in the neighborhood. There I lay prone and helpless, wondering if it would not be strictly just that they should come and tear me to pieces. I heard them calling for a long time before I realized that dim, shadowy forms were sneaking near. The horse saw them first, and his terrified snort drove them back at first, but they came nearer next time and sat around me on the prairie. Soon one bolder than the others crawled up and tugged at the body of his dead relative. I shouted and he retreated growling. The pony ran to a distance in terror. Presently the wolf returned, and after two or three of these retreats and returns, the body was dragged off and devoured by the rest in a few minutes.

After this they gathered nearer and sat on their haunches to look at me, and the boldest one smelt the rifle and scratched dirt on it. He retreated when I kicked at him with my free foot and shouted, but growing bolder as I grew weaker he came and snarled right in my face. At this several others snarled and came up closer, and I realized that I was to be devoured by the foe that I most despised, when suddenly out of the gloom with a guttural roar sprang a great black wolf. The prairie wolves scattered like chaff except the bold one, which seized by the black new-comer was in a few moments a draggled corpse, and then, oh horrors ! this mighty brute bounded at me and— Bingo—noble Bingo, rubbed his shaggy, panting sides against me and licked my cold face.

" Bingo—Bing—old—boy — Fetch me the trap-wrench ! "

Away he went and returned dragging the rifle, for he knew only that I wanted something.

" No—Bing—the trap-wrench." This time it was my sash, but at last he brought the wrench and wagged his tail in joy that it was right. Reaching out with my free hand, after much difficulty I unscrewed the pillar-nut. The trap fell apart and my hand was released, and a minute later I was free. Bing brought the pony up, and after slowly walking to restore the circulation I was able to mount. Then slowly at first but soon at a gallop, with Bingo as herald careering and barking ahead, we set out for home, there to learn that the night before, though never taken on the trapping rounds, the brave dog had acted strangely, whimpering and watching the timber-trail; and at last when night came on, in spite of attempts to detain him he had set out in the gloom and guided by a knowledge that is beyond us had reached the spot in time to avenge me as well as set me free.

Stanch old Bing—he was a strange dog. Though his heart was with me, he passed me next day with scarcely a look, but responded with alacrity when little Gordon called him to a gopher-hunt. And it was so to the end; and to the end also he lived the wolfish life that he loved, and never failed to seek the winter-killed horses and found one again with a poisoned bait, and wolfishly bolted that; then feeling the pang, set out, not for Wright's but to find me, and reached the door of my shanty where I should have been. Next day on returning I found him dead in the snow with his head on the sill of the door—the door of his puppyhood's days; my dog to the last in his heart of hearts — it was my help he sought, and vainly sought, in the hour of his bitter extremity.

The
Springfield Fox

The Springfield Fox

I

THE hens had been mysteriously disappearing for over a month; and when I came home to Springfield for the summer holidays it was my duty to find the cause. This was soon done. The fowls were carried away bodily one at a time, before going to roost or else after leaving, which put tramps and neighbors out of court; they were not taken from the high perches, which cleared all coons and owls; or left partly eaten, so that weasels, skunks, or minks were not the guilty ones, and the blame, therefore, was surely left at Reynard's door.

The great pine wood of Erindale was on the other bank of the river, and on looking care-

fully about the lower ford I saw a few fox-tracks and a barred feather from one of our Plymouth Rock chickens. On climbing the farther bank in search of more clews, I heard a great outcry of crows behind me, and turning, saw a number of these birds darting down at something in the ford. A better view showed that it was the old story, thief catch thief, for there in the middle of the ford was a fox with something in his jaws—he was returning from our barnyard with another hen. The crows, though shameless robbers themselves, are ever first to cry 'Stop thief,' and yet more than ready to take 'hush-money' in the form of a share in the plunder.

And this was their game now. The fox to get back home must cross the river, where he was exposed to the full brunt of the crow mob. He made a dash for it, and would doubtless have gotten across with his booty had I not joined in the attack, whereupon he dropped the hen, scarce dead, and disappeared in the woods.

This large and regular levy of provisions wholly carried off could mean but one thing, a family of little foxes at home ; and to find them I now was bound.

The Springfield Fox

That evening I went with Ranger, my hound, across the river into the Erindale woods. As soon as the hound began to circle, we heard the short, sharp bark of a fox from a thickly wooded ravine close by. Ranger dashed in at once, struck a hot scent and went off on a lively straight-away till his voice was lost in the distance away over the upland.

After nearly an hour he came back, panting and warm, for it was baking August weather, and lay down at my feet.

But almost immediately the same foxy '*Yap yurrr*' was heard close at hand and off dashed the dog on another chase.

Away he went in the darkness, baying like a foghorn, straight away to the north. And the loud '*Boo, boo,*' became a low '*oo, oo,*' and that a feeble '*o-o*' and then was lost. They must have gone some miles away, for even with ear to the ground I heard nothing of them though a mile was easy distance for Ranger's brazen voice.

As I waited in the black woods I heard a sweet sound of dripping water : '*Tink tank tenk tink, Ta tink tank tenk tonk.*'

The Springfield Fox

I did not know of any spring so near, and in the hot night it was a glad find. But the sound led me to the bough of an oak-tree, where I found its source. Such a soft sweet song; full of delightful suggestion on such a night:

Tonk tank tenk tink
Ta tink a tonk a tank a tink a
Ta ta tink tank ta ta tonk tink
Drink a tank a drink a drunk.

It was the 'water-dripping' song of the saw-whet owl.

But suddenly a deep raucous breathing and a rustle of leaves showed that Ranger was back. He was completely fagged out. His tongue hung almost to the ground and was dripping with foam, his flanks were heaving and spume-flecks dribbled from his breast and sides. He stopped panting a moment to give my hand a dutiful lick, then flung himself flop on the leaves to drown all other sounds with his noisy panting.

But again that tantalizing '*Yap yurrr*' was heard a few feet away, and the meaning of it all dawned on me.

We were close to the den where the little

foxes were, and the old ones were taking turns in trying to lead us away.

It was late night now, so we went home feeling sure that the problem was nearly solved.

II

It was well known that there was an old fox with his family living in the neighborhood, but no one supposed them so near.

This fox had been called 'Scarface,' because of a scar reaching from his eye through and back of his ear ; this was supposed to have been given him by a barbed-wire fence during a rabbit hunt, and as the hair came in white after it healed, it was always a strong mark.

The winter before I had met with him and had had a sample of his craftiness. I was out shooting, after a fall of snow, and had crossed the open fields to the edge of the brushy hollow back of the old mill. As my head rose to a view of the hollow I caught sight of a fox trotting at long range down the other side, in line to cross my course. Instantly I held motionless, and did not even lower or turn my

153

head lest I should catch his eye by moving, until he went on out of sight in the thick cover at the bottom. As soon as he was hidden I bobbed down and ran to head him off where he should leave the cover on the other side, and was there in good time awaiting, but no fox came forth. A careful look showed the fresh track of a fox that had bounded from the cover, and following it with my eye I saw old Scarface himself far out of range behind me, sitting on his haunches and grinning as though much amused.

A study of the trail made all clear. He had seen me at the moment I saw him, but he, also like a true hunter, had concealed the fact, putting on an air of unconcern till out of sight, when he had run for his life around behind me and amused himself by watching my stillborn trick.

In the springtime I had yet another instance of Scarface's cunning. I was walking with a friend along the road over the high pasture. We passed within thirty feet of a ridge on which were several gray and brown bowlders. When at the nearest point my friend said :

The Springfield Fox

" Stone number three looks to me very much like a fox curled up.''

But I could not see it, and we passed. We had not gone many yards farther when the wind blew on this bowlder as on fur.

My friend said, " I am sure that is a fox, lying asleep.''

" We'll soon settle that," I replied, and turned back, but as soon as I had taken one step from the road, up jumped Scarface, for it was he, and ran. A fire had swept the middle of the pasture, leaving a broad belt of black; over this he skurried till he came to the unburnt yellow grass again, where he squatted down and was lost to view. He had been watching us all the time, and would not have moved had we kept to the road. The wonderful part of this is, not that he resembled the round stones and dry grass, but that he *knew he did*, and was ready to profit by it.

We soon found that it was Scarface and his wife Vixen that had made our woods their home and our barnyard their base of supplies.

Next morning a search in the pines showed a great bank of earth that had been scratched up within a few months. It must have come from a hole, and yet there was none to be seen. It is well known that a really cute fox, on digging a new den, brings all the earth out at the first hole made, but carries on a tunnel into some distant thicket. Then closing up for good the first made and too well-marked door, uses only the entrance hidden in the thicket.

So after a little search at the other side of a knoll, I found the real entry and good proof that there was a nest of little foxes inside.

Rising above the brush on the hillside was a great hollow basswood. It leaned a good deal and had a large hole at the bottom, and a smaller one at top.

We boys had often used this tree in playing Swiss Family Robinson, and by cutting steps in its soft punky walls had made it easy to go up and down in the hollow. Now it came in handy, for next day when the sun was warm I went there to watch, and from this perch on the roof, I soon saw the interesting family that lived in the cellar near by. There were four little foxes; they looked curiously like little lambs, with their woolly coats, their long thick legs and innocent expressions, and yet a second glance at their broad, sharp-nosed, sharp-eyed visages showed that each of these innocents was the makings of a crafty old fox.

They played about, basking in the sun, or wrestling with each other till a slight sound made them skurry under ground. But their alarm was needless, for the cause of it was their mother; she stepped from the bushes bringing another hen—number seventeen as I remember. A low call from her and the little fellows came tumbling out. Then began a scene that I thought charming, but which my uncle would not have enjoyed at all.

They rushed on the hen, and tussled and fought with it, and each other, while the mother, keeping a sharp eye for enemies, looked on with fond delight. The expression on her face was remarkable. It was first a grinning of delight, but her usual look of wildness and cunning was there, nor were cruelty and nervousness lacking, but over all was the unmistakable look of the mother's pride and love.

The base of my tree was hidden in bushes and much lower than the knoll where the den

was. So I could come and go at will without scaring the foxes.

For many days I went there and saw much of the training of the young ones. They early learned to turn to statuettes at any strange sound, and then on hearing it again or finding other cause for fear, to run for shelter.

Some animals have so much mother-love that it overflows and benefits outsiders. Not so old Vixen it would seem. Her pleasure in the cubs led to most refined cruelty. For she often brought home to them mice and birds alive, and with diabolic gentleness would avoid doing them serious hurt so that the cubs might have larger scope to torment them.

There was a woodchuck that lived over in the hill orchard. He was neither handsome nor interesting, but he knew how to take care of himself. He had digged a den between the roots of an old pine stump, so that the foxes could not follow him by digging. But hard work was not their way of life; wits they believed worth more than elbow-grease. This woodchuck usually sunned himself on the stump each morning. If he saw a fox near he went

158

down in the door of his den, or if the enemy was very near he went inside and stayed long enough for the danger to pass.

One morning Vixen and her mate seemed to decide that it was time the children knew something about the broad subject of Woodchucks, and further that this orchard woodchuck would serve nicely for an object-lesson. So they went together to the orchard-fence unseen by old Chuckie on his stump. Scarface then showed himself in the orchard and quietly walked in a line so as to pass by the stump at a distance, but never once turned his head or allowed the ever-watchful woodchuck to think himself seen. When the fox entered the field the woodchuck quietly dropped down to the mouth of his den ; here he waited as the fox passed, but concluding that after all wisdom is the better part, went into his hole.

This was what the foxes wanted. Vixen had kept out of sight, but now ran swiftly to the stump and hid behind it. Scarface had kept straight on, going very slowly. The woodchuck had not been frightened, so before long his head popped up between the roots and he looked

159

around. There was that fox still going on, farther and farther away. The woodchuck grew bold as the fox went, and came out farther, and then seeing the coast clear, he scrambled onto the stump, and with one spring Vixen had him and shook him till he lay senseless. Scarface had watched out of the corner of his eye and now came running back. But Vixen took the chuck in her jaws and made for the den, so he saw he wasn't needed.

Back to the den came Vix, and carried the chuck so carefully that he was able to struggle a little when she got there. A low '*woof*' at the den brought the little fellows out like schoolboys to play. She threw the wounded animal to them and they set on him like four little furies, uttering little growls and biting little bites with all the strength of their baby jaws, but the woodchuck fought for his life and beating them off slowly hobbled to the shelter of a thicket. The little ones pursued like a pack of hounds and dragged at his tail and flanks, but could not hold him back. So Vix overtook him with a couple of bounds and dragged him again into the open for the children to worry.

The Springfield Fox

Again and again this rough sport went on till one of the little ones was badly bitten, and his squeal of pain roused Vix to end the woodchuck's misery and serve him up at once.

Not far from the den was a hollow overgrown with coarse grass, the playground of a colony of field-mice. The earliest lesson in woodcraft that the little ones took, away from the den, was in this hollow. Here they had their first course of mice, the easiest of all game. In teaching, the main thing was example, aided by a deep-set instinct. The old fox, also, had one or two signs meaning "lie still and watch," "come, do as I do," and so on, that were much used.

So the merry lot went to this hollow one calm evening and Mother Fox made them lie still in the grass. Presently a faint squeak showed that the game was astir. Vix rose up and went on tip-toe into the grass—not crouching but as high as she could stand, sometimes on her hind legs so as to get a better view. The runs that the mice follow are hidden under the grass tangle, and the only way to know the whereabouts of a mouse is by seeing the slight shaking of the grass, which is the reason why mice are hunted only on calm days.

And the trick is to locate the mouse and seize him first and see him afterward. Vix soon made a spring, and in the middle of the bunch of dead grass that she grabbed was a field-mouse squeaking his last squeak.

He was soon gobbled, and the four awkward little foxes tried to do the same as their mother, and when at length the eldest for the first time in his life caught game, he quivered with excitement and ground his pearly little milk-teeth into the mouse with a rush of inborn savageness that must have surprised even himself.

Another home lesson was on the red-squirrel. One of these noisy, vulgar creatures, lived close by and used to waste part of each day scolding the foxes, from some safe perch. The cubs made many vain attempts to catch him as he ran across their glade from one tree to another, or spluttered and scolded at them a foot or so out of reach. But old Vixen was up in natural history—she knew squirrel nature and took the case in hand when the proper time came. She hid the children and lay down flat in the middle of the open glade. The saucy low-minded squirrel came and scolded as usual. But she moved no hair. He came nearer and at last right overhead to chatter :

" You brute you, you brute you."

But Vix lay as dead. This was very perplexing, so the squirrel came down the trunk and peeping about made a nervous dash across the grass, to another tree, again to scold from a safe perch.

" You brute you, you useless brute, scarrr-scarrrrr."

But flat and lifeless on the grass lay Vix. This was most tantalizing to the squirrel. He was naturally curious and disposed to be venturesome, so again he came to the ground and skurried across the glade nearer than before.

Still as death lay Vix, " surely she was dead." And the little foxes began to wonder if their mother wasn't asleep.

But the squirrel was working himself into a little craze of foolhardy curiosity. He had dropped a piece of bark on Vix's head, he had used up his list of bad words and he had done it all over again, without getting a sign of life.

The Springfield Fox

So after a couple more dashes across the glade he ventured within a few feet of the really watchful Vix, who sprang to her feet and pinned him in a twinkling.

"And the little ones picked the bones e-oh."

Thus the rudiments of their education were laid, and afterward as they grew stronger they were taken farther afield to begin the higher branches of trailing and scenting.

For each kind of prey they were taught a way to hunt, for every animal has some great strength or it could not live, and some great weakness or the others could not live. The squirrel's weakness was foolish curiosity; the fox's that he can't climb a tree. And the training of the little foxes was all shaped to take advantage of the weakness of the other creatures and to make up for their own by defter play where they are strong.

From their parents they learned the chief axioms of the fox world. How, is not easy to say. But that they learned this in company with their parents was clear. Here are some that foxes taught me, without saying a word:—

Never sleep on your straight track.

'And the little ones picked his Bones e-oh!'

The Springfield Fox

Your nose is before your eyes, then trust it first.

A fool runs down the wind.

Running rills cure many ills.

Never take the open if you can keep the cover.

Never leave a straight trail if a crooked one will do.

If it's strange, it's hostile.

Dust and water burn the scent.

Never hunt mice in a rabbit-woods, or rabbits in a henyard.

Keep off the grass.

Inklings of the meanings of these were already entering the little ones' minds—thus, ' Never follow what you can't smell,' was wise, they could see, because if you can't smell it, then the wind is so that it must smell you.

One by one they learned the birds and beasts of their home woods, and then as they were able to go abroad with their parents they learned new animals. They were beginning to think they knew the scent of everything that moved. But one night the mother took them to a field where was a strange black flat thing on the

ground.   She brought them on purpose to
smell it, but at the first whiff their every hair
stood on end, they trembled, they knew not
why—it seemed to tingle through their blood
and fill them with instinctive hate and fear.
And when she saw its full effect she told them—
"That is man-scent."

III

Meanwhile the hens continued to disappear.
I had not betrayed the den of cubs.   Indeed,
I thought a good deal more of the little rascals
than I did of the hens ; but uncle was dreadfully wrought up and made most disparaging
remarks about my woodcraft.   To please him
I one day took the hound across to the woods
and seating myself on a stump on the open hill-
side, I bade the dog go on.   Within three minutes he sang out in the tongue all hunters know
so well, "Fox ! fox ! fox ! straight away down
the valley."

After awhile I heard them coming back.
There I saw the fox—Scarface—loping lightly
across the river-bottom to the stream.   In he

went and trotted along in the shallow water near the margin for two hundred yards, then came out straight toward me. Though in full view, he saw me not but came up the hill watching over his shoulder for the hound. Within ten feet of me he turned and sat with his back to me while he craned his neck and showed an eager interest in the doings of the hound. Ranger came bawling along the trail till he came to the running water, the killer of scent, and here he was puzzled ; but there was only one thing to do ; that was by going up and down both banks find where the fox had left the river.

The fox before me shifted his position a little to get a better view and watched with a most human interest all the circling of the hound. He was so close that I saw the hair of his shoulder bristle a little when the dog came in sight. I could see the jumping of his heart on his ribs, and the gleam of his yellow eye. When the dog was wholly baulked by the water trick, it was comical to see :—he could not sit still, but rocked up and down in glee, and reared on his hind feet to get a better view of the slow-plodding hound. With mouth opened nearly to his ears, though not at all winded, he panted noisily for a moment, or rather he laughed gleefully, just as a dog laughs by grinning and panting.

Old Scarface wriggled in huge enjoyment as the hound puzzled over the trail so long that when he did find it, it was so stale he could barely follow it, and did not feel justified in tonguing on it at all.

As soon as the hound was working up the hill, the fox quietly went into the woods. I had been sitting in plain view only ten feet away, but I had the wind and kept still and the fox never knew that his life had for twenty minutes been in the power of the foe he most feared. Ranger also would have passed me as near as the fox, but I spoke to him, and with a little nervous start he quit the trail and looking sheepish lay down by my feet.

This little comedy was played with variations for several days, but it was all in plain view from the house across the river. My uncle, impatient at the daily loss of hens, went out himself, sat on the open knoll, and when old Scar-

face trotted to his lookout to watch the dull
hound on the river flat below, my uncle remorse-
lessly shot him in the back, at the very moment
when he was grinning over a new triumph.

IV

But still the hens were disappearing. My
uncle was wrathy. He determined to conduct
the war himself, and sowed the woods with
poison baits, trusting to luck that our own dogs
would not get them. He indulged in contemptu-
ous remarks on my by-gone woodcraft, and went
out evenings with a gun and the two dogs, to see
what he could destroy.

Vix knew right well what a poisoned bait was;
she passed them by or else treated them with
active contempt, but one she dropped down
the hole of an old enemy, a skunk, who was
never afterward seen. Formerly old Scarface
was always ready to take charge of the dogs,
and keep them out of mischief. But now that
Vix had the whole burden of the brood, she
could no longer spend time in breaking every
track to the den, and was not always at hand

169

to meet and mislead the foes that might be coming too near.

The end is easily foreseen. Ranger followed a hot trail to the den, and Spot, the fox-terrier, announced that the family was at home, and then did his best to go in after them.

The whole secret was now out, and the whole family doomed. The hired man came around with pick and shovel to dig them out, while we and the dogs stood by. Old Vix soon showed herself in the near woods, and led the dogs away off down the river, where she shook them off when she thought proper, by the simple device of springing on a sheep's back. The frightened animal ran for several hundred yards, then Vix got off, knowing that there was now a hopeless gap in the scent, and returned to the den. But the dogs, baffled by the break in the trail, soon did the same, to find Vix hanging about in despair, vainly trying to decoy us away from her treasures.

Meanwhile Paddy plied both pick and shovel with vigor and effect. The yellow, gravelly sand was heaping on both sides, and the shoulders of the sturdy digger were sinking below the level.

The Springfield Fox

After an hour's digging, enlivened by frantic rushes of the dogs after the old fox, who hovered near in the woods, Pat called :

"Here they are, sor ! "

It was the den at the end of the burrow, and cowering as far back as they could, were the four little woolly cubs.

Before I could interfere, a murderous blow from the shovel, and a sudden rush for the fierce little terrier, ended the lives of three. The fourth and smallest was barely saved by holding him by his tail high out of reach of the excited dogs.

He gave one short squeal, and his poor mother came at the cry, and circled so near that she would have been shot but for the accidental protection of the dogs, who somehow always seemed to get between, and whom she once more led away on a fruitless chase.

The little one saved alive was dropped into a bag, where he lay quite still. His unfortunate brothers were thrown back into their nursery bed, and buried under a few shovelfuls of earth.

We guilty ones then went back into the house, and the little fox was soon chained in the yard. No one knew just why he was kept alive, but in all a change of feeling had set in, and the idea of killing him was without a supporter.

He was a pretty little fellow, like a cross between a fox and a lamb. His woolly visage and form were strangely lamb-like and innocent, but one could find in his yellow eyes a gleam of cunning and savageness as unlamb-like as it possibly could be.

As long as anyone was near he crouched sullen and cowed in his shelter-box, and it was a full hour after being left alone before he ventured to look out.

My window now took the place of the hollow basswood. A number of hens of the breed he knew so well were about the cub in the the yard. Late that afternoon as they strayed near the captive there was a sudden rattle of the chain, and the youngster dashed at the nearest one and would have caught him but for the chain which brought him up with a jerk. He got on his feet and slunk back to his box, and though he afterward made several rushes he so gauged his leap as to win or fail within the

length of the chain and never again was brought
up by its cruel jerk.

As night came down the little fellow became
very uneasy, sneaking out of his box, but going
back at each slight alarm, tugging at his chain,
or at times biting it in fury while he held it
down with his fore paws. Suddenly he paused
as though listening, then raising his little black
nose he poured out a short quavering cry.

Once or twice this was repeated, the time
between being occupied in worrying the chain
and running about. Then an answer came.
The far-away *Yap-yurrr* of the old fox. A
few minutes later a shadowy form appeared on
the wood-pile. The little one slunk into his
box, but at once returned and ran to meet his
mother with all the gladness that a fox could
show. Quick as a flash she seized him and
turned to bear him away by the road she came.
But the moment the end of the chain was
reached the cub was rudely jerked from the old
one's mouth, and she, scared by the opening of
a window, fled over the wood-pile.

An hour afterward the cub had ceased to run
about or cry. I peeped out, and by the light

173

Slunk back into his box

of the moon saw the form of the mother at full
length on the ground by the little one, gnawing at something—the clank of iron told what,
it was that cruel chain. And Tip, the little
one, meanwhile was helping himself to a warm
drink.

On my going out she fled into the dark
woods, but there by the shelter-box were two
little mice, bloody and still warm, food for the
cub brought by the devoted mother. And in
the morning I found the chain was very bright
for a foot or two next the little one's collar.

On walking across the woods to the ruined
den, I again found signs of Vixen. The poor
heart-broken mother had come and dug out the
bedraggled bodies of her little ones.

There lay the three little baby foxes all
licked smooth now, and by them were two of
our hens fresh killed. The newly heaved earth
was printed all over with tell-tale signs—signs
that told me that here by the side of her dead
she had watched like Rizpah. Here she had
brought their usual meal, the spoil of her nightly hunt. Here she had stretched herself beside them and vainly offered them their natural

drink and yearned to feed and warm them as of old ; but only stiff little bodies under their soft wool she found, and little cold noses still and unresponsive.

A deep impress of elbows, breast, and hocks showed where she had laid in silent grief and watched them for long and mourned as a wild mother can mourn for its young. But from that time she came no more to the ruined den, for now she surely knew that her little ones were dead.

V

Tip the captive, the weakling of the brood, was now the heir to all her love. The dogs were loosed to guard the hens. The hired  man had orders to shoot the old fox on sight— so had I, but was resolved never to see her. Chicken-heads, that a fox loves and a dog will not touch, had been poisoned and scattered through the woods ; and the only way to the yard where Tip was tied, was by climbing the wood-pile after braving all other dangers. And yet each night old Vix was there to nurse her

baby and bring it fresh-killed hens and game. Again and again I saw her, although she came now without awaiting the querulous cry of the captive.

The second night of the captivity I heard the rattle of the chain, and then made out that the old fox was there, hard at work digging a hole by the little one's kennel. When it was deep enough to half bury her, she gathered into it all the slack of the chain, and filled it again with earth. Then in triumph thinking she had gotten rid of the chain, she seized little Tip by the neck and turned to dash off up the wood-pile, but alas only to have him jerked roughly from her grasp.

Poor little fellow, he whimpered sadly as he crawled into his box. After half an hour there was a great outcry among the dogs, and by their straight-away tonguing through the far woods I knew they were chasing Vix. Away up north they went in the direction of the railway and their noise faded from hearing. Next morning the hound had not come back. We soon knew why. Foxes long ago learned what a railroad is; they soon devised several ways of turning it to account. One way is when hunted to walk the rails for a long distance just before a train comes. The scent, always poor on iron, is destroyed by the train and there is always a chance of hounds being killed by the engine. But another way more sure, but harder to play, is to lead the hounds straight to a high trestle just ahead of the train, so that the engine overtakes them on it and they are surely dashed to destruction.

This trick was skilfully played, and down below we found the mangled remains of old Ranger and learned that Vix was already wreaking her revenge.

That same night she returned to the yard before Spot's weary limbs could bring him back and killed another hen and brought it to Tip, and stretched her panting length beside him that he might quench his thirst. For she seemed to think he had no food but what she brought.

It was that hen that betrayed to my uncle the nightly visits.

My own sympathies were all turning to Vix, and I would have no hand in planning further murders. Next night my uncle himself watched, gun in hand, for an hour. Then when it became cold and the moon clouded over he remembered other important business elsewhere, and left Paddy in his place.

But Paddy was "onaisy" as the stillness and anxiety of watching worked on his nerves. And the loud bang! bang! an hour later left us sure only that powder had been burned.

In the morning we found Vix had not failed her young one. Again next night found my uncle on guard, for another hen had been taken. Soon after dark a single shot was heard, but Vix dropped the game she was bringing and escaped. Another attempt made that night called forth another gun-shot. Yet next day it was seen by the brightness of the chain that she had come again and vainly tried for hours to cut that hateful bond.

Such courage and stanch fidelity were bound to win respect, if not toleration. At any rate, there was no gunner in wait next night, when all was still. Could it be of any use? Driven off thrice with gun-shots, would she make another try to feed or free her captive young one?

The Springfield Fox

Would she? Hers was a mother's love. There was but one to watch them this time, the fourth night, when the quavering whine of the little one was followed by that shadowy form above the wood-pile.

But carrying no fowl or food that could be seen. Had the keen huntress failed at last? Had she no head of game for this her only charge, or had she learned to trust his captors for his food?

No, far from all this. The wild-wood mother's heart and hate were true. Her only thought had been to set him free. All means she knew she tried, and every danger braved to tend him well and help him to be free. But all had failed.

Like a shadow she came and in a moment was gone, and Tip seized on something dropped, and crunched and chewed with relish what she brought. But even as he ate, a knife-like pang shot through and a scream of pain escaped him. Then there was a momentary struggle and the little fox was dead.

The mother's love was strong in Vix, but a higher thought was stronger. She knew right

179

well the poison's power; she knew the poison
bait, and would have taught him had he lived
to know and shun it too. But now at last
when she must choose for him a wretched prisoner's life or sudden death, she quenched the
mother in her breast and freed him by the one
remaining door.

.   .   .   .

It is when the snow is on the ground that
we take the census of the woods, and when the
winter came it told me that Vix no longer
roamed the woods of Erindale. Where she
went it never told, but only this, that she was
gone.

Gone, perhaps, to some other far-off haunt
to leave behind the sad remembrance of her
murdered little ones and mate. Or gone, may
be, deliberately, from the scene of a sorrowful
life, as many a wild-wood mother has gone, by
the means that she herself had used to free her
young one, the last of all her brood.

The Pacing Mustang

The Pacing Mustang

I

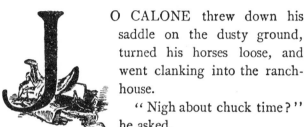

JO CALONE threw down his saddle on the dusty ground, turned his horses loose, and went clanking into the ranchhouse.

" Nigh about chuck time ? " he asked.

" Seventeen minutes," said the cook glancing at the Waterbury, with the air of a train-starter, though this show of precision had never yet been justified by events.

" How's things on the Perico ? " said Jo's pard.

" Hotter'n hinges," said Jo. " Cattle seem O. K.; lots of calves."

. . . . .

" I seen that bunch o' mustangs that waters at Antelope Springs; couple o' colts along; one little dark one, a fair dandy; a born pacer. I run them a mile or two, and he led the bunch, an' never broke his pace. Cut loose, an' pushed them jest for fun, an' darned if I could make him break."

" You didn't have no reefreshments along ? " said Scarth, incredulously.

" That's all right, Scarth. You had to crawl on our last bet, an' you'll get another chance soon as you're man enough."

" Chuck," shouted the cook, and the subject was dropped. Next day the scene of the round-up was changed, and the mustangs were forgotten.

A year later the same corner of New Mexico was worked over by the roundup, and again the mustang bunch was seen. The dark colt was now a black yearling, with thin, clean legs and glossy flanks; and more than one of the boys saw with his own eyes this oddity—the mustang was a born pacer.

Jo was along, and the idea now struck him that that colt was worth having. To an Easterner this thought may not seem startling or original, but in the West, where an unbroken horse is worth $5, and where an ordinary saddle-horse is worth $15 or $20, the idea of a wild mustang being desirable property does not occur to the average cowboy, for mustangs are hard to catch, and when caught are merely wild animal prisoners, perfectly useless and untamable to the last. Not a few of the cattle-owners make a point of shooting all mustangs at sight, for they are not only useless cumberers of the feeding-grounds, but commonly lead away domestic horses, which soon take to the wild life and are thenceforth lost.

Wild Jo Calone knew a ' bronk right down to subsoil.' " I never seen a white that wasn't soft, nor a chestnut that wasn't nervous, nor a bay that wasn't good if broke right, nor a black that wasn't hard as nails, an' full of the old Harry. All a black bronk wants is claws to be wus'n Daniel's hull outfit of lions."

Since then a mustang is worthless vermin, and a black mustang ten times worse than worth-less, Jo's pard " didn't see no sense in Jo's wantin' to corral the yearling," as he now

seemed intent on doing. But Jo got no chance
to try that year.

He was only a cow-puncher on $25 a month,
and tied to hours. Like most of the boys, he
always looked forward to having a ranch and
an outfit of his own. His brand, the hogpen,
of sinister suggestion, was already registered at
Santa Fé, but of horned stock it was borne by
a single old cow, so as to give him a legal right
to put his brand on any maverick (or unbranded
animal) he might chance to find.

Yet each fall, when paid off, Jo could not resist the temptation to go to town with the boys
and have a good time ' while the stuff held out.'
So that his property consisted of little more
than his saddle, his bed, and his old cow. He
kept on hoping to make a strike that would
leave him well fixed with a fair start, and when
the thought came that the Black Mustang was
his mascot, he only needed a chance to 'make
the try.'

The roundup circled down to the Canadian
River, and back in the fall by the Don Carlos
Hills, and Jo saw no more of the Pacer, though
he heard of him from many quarters, for the

colt, now a vigorous, young horse, rising three, was beginning to be talked of.

Antelope Springs is in the middle of a great level plain. When the water is high it spreads into a small lake with a belt of sedge around it; when it is low there is a wide flat of black mud, glistening white with alkali in places, and the spring a water-hole in the middle. It has no flow or outlet and yet is fairly good water, the only drinking-place for many miles.

This flat, or prairie as it would be called farther north, was the favorite feeding-ground of the Black Stallion, but it was also the pasture of many herds of range horses and cattle. Chiefly interested was the ' L cross F ' outfit. Foster, the manager and part owner, was a man of enterprise. He believed it would pay to handle a better class of cattle and horses on the range, and one of his ventures was ten half-blooded mares, tall, clean-limbed, deer-eyed creatures, that made the scrub cow-ponies look like pitiful starvelings of some degenerate and quite different species.

One of these was kept stabled for use, but the nine, after the weaning of their colts, managed to get away and wandered off on the range.

A horse has a fine instinct for the road to the best feed, and the nine mares drifted, of course, to the prairie of Antelope Springs, twenty miles to the southward. And when, later that summer Foster went to round them up, he found the nine indeed, but with them and guarding them with an air of more than mere comradeship was a coal-black stallion, prancing around and rounding up the bunch like an expert, his jet-black coat a vivid contrast to the golden hides of his harem.

The mares were gentle, and would have been easily driven homeward but for a new and unexpected thing. The Black Stallion became greatly aroused. He seemed to inspire them too with his wildness, and flying this way and that way drove the whole band at full gallop where he would. Away they went, and the little cowponies that carried the men were easily left behind.

This was maddening, and both men at last drew their guns and sought a chance to drop that ' blasted stallion.' But no chance came that was not 9 to 1 of dropping one of the mares. A long day of manœuvring made no change. The Pacer, for it was he, kept his family together and disappeared among the southern sandhills. The cattlemen on their jaded ponies set out for home with the poor satisfaction of vowing vengeance for their failure on the superb cause of it.

One of the most aggravating parts of it was that one or two experiences like this would surely make the mares as wild as the Mustang, and there seemed to be no way of saving them from it.

Scientists differ on the power of beauty and prowess to attract female admiration among the lower animals, but whether it is admiration or the prowess itself, it is certain that a wild animal of uncommon gifts soon wins a large following from the harems of his rivals. And the great Black Horse, with his inky mane and tail and his green-lighted eyes, ranged through all that region and added to his following from many bands till not less than a score of mares were in his ' bunch.' Most were merely humble cow-ponies turned out to range, but the nine great mares were there, a striking group by themselves. According to all reports, this bunch was always kept rounded up and guarded with such energy and jealousy that a mare, once in it, was a lost animal so far as man was concerned, and the ranchmen realized soon that they had gotten on the range a mustang that was doing them more harm than all other sources of loss put together.

II

It was December, 1893. I was new in the country, and was setting out from the ranch-house on the Pinavetitos, to go with a wagon to the Canadian River. As I was leaving, Foster finished his remark by: "And if you get a chance to draw a bead on that accursed mustang, don't fail to drop him in his tracks."

This was the first I had heard of him, and as I rode along I gathered from Burns, my guide, the history that has been given. I was full of curiosity to see the famous three-year-old, and

was not a little disappointed on the second day
when we came to the prairie on Antelope
Springs and saw no sign of the Pacer or his band.

But on the next day, as we crossed the Alamosa Arroyo, and were rising to the rolling
prairie again, Jack Burns, who was riding on
ahead, suddenly dropped flat on the neck of his
horse, and swung back to me in the wagon,
saying :

"Get out your rifle, here's that —— stallion."

I seized my rifle, and hurried forward to a
view over the prairie ridge.   In the hollow below was a band of horses, and there at one end
was the Great Black Mustang.   He had heard
some sound of our approach, and was not un-
suspicious of danger.   There he stood with
head and tail erect, and nostrils wide, an image
of horse perfection and beauty, as noble an
animal as ever ranged the plains, and the mere
notion of turning that magnificent creature into
a mass of carrion was horrible.   In spite of
Jack's exhortation to 'shoot quick,' I delayed,
and threw open the breach, whereupon he, always hot and hasty, swore at my slowness,
growled, ' Gi' me that gun,' and as he seized

it I turned the muzzle up, and *accidentally* the gun went off.

Instantly the herd below was all alarm, the great black leader snorted and neighed and dashed about. And the mares bunched, and away all went in a rumble of hoofs, and a cloud of dust.

The Stallion careered now on this side, now on that, and kept his eye on all and led and drove them far away. As long as I could see I watched, and never once did he break his pace.

Jack made Western remarks about me and my gun, as well as that mustang, but I rejoiced in the Pacer's strength and beauty, and not for all the mares in the bunch would I have harmed his glossy hide.

III

There are several ways of capturing wild horses. One is by creasing—that is, grazing the animal's nape with a rifle-ball so that he is stunned long enough for hobbling.

"Yes! I seen about a hundred necks broke

192

trying it, but I never seen a mustang creased yet," was Wild Jo's critical remark.

Sometimes, if the shape of the country abets it, the herd can be driven into a corral ; sometimes with extra fine mounts they can be run down, but by far the commonest way, paradoxical as it may seem, is to *walk* them down.

The fame of the Stallion that never was known to gallop was spreading. Extraordinary stories were told of his gait, his speed, and his wind, and when old Montgomery of the 'triangle-bar' outfit came out plump at Well's Hotel in Clayton, and in presence of witnesses said he'd give one thousand dollars cash for him safe in a box-car, providing the stories were true, a dozen young cow-punchers were eager to cut loose and win the purse, as soon as present engagements were up. But Wild Jo had had his eye on this very deal for quite a while ; there was no time to lose, so ignoring present contracts he rustled all night to raise the necessary equipment for the game.

By straining his already overstrained credit, and taxing the already overtaxed generosity of his friends, he got together an expedition consisting of twenty good saddle-horses, a mess-wagon, and a fortnight's stuff for three men—himself, his ' pard,' Charley, and the cook.

Then they set out from Clayton, with the avowed intention of walking down the wonderfully swift wild horse. The third day they arrived at Antelope Springs, and as it was about noon they were not surprised to see the black Pacer marching down to drink with all his band behind him. Jo kept out of sight until the wild horses each and all had drunk their fill, for a thirsty animal always travels better than one laden with water.

Jo then rode quietly forward. The Pacer took alarm at half a mile, and led his band away out of sight on the soapweed mesa to the southeast. Jo followed at a gallop till he once more sighted them, then came back and instructed the cook, who was also teamster, to make for Alamosa Arroyo in the south. Then away to the southeast he went after the mustangs. After a mile or two he once more sighted them, and walked his horse quietly till so near that they again took alarm and circled away to the south. An hour's trot, not on the trail, but cutting

The Pacing Mustang

across to where they ought to go, brought Jo
again in close sight. Again he walked quietly
toward the herd, and again there was the alarm
and flight. And so they passed the afternoon,
but circled ever more and more to the south, so
that when the sun was low they were, as Jo had
expected, not far from Alamosa Arroyo. The
band was again close at hand, and Jo, after
starting them off, rode to the wagon, while his
pard, who had been taking it easy, took up the
slow chase on a fresh horse.

After supper the wagon moved on to the up-
per ford of the Alamosa, as arranged, and there
camped for the night.

Meanwhile, Charley followed the herd. They
had not run so far as at first, for their pursuer
made no sign of attack, and they were getting
used to his company. They were more easily
found, as the shadows fell, on account of a snow-
white mare that was in the bunch. A young
moon in the sky now gave some help, and rely-
ing on his horse to choose the path, Charley kept
him quietly walking after the herd, represented
by that ghost-white mare, till they were lost in
the night. He then got off, unsaddled and

picketed his horse, and in his blanket quickly
went to sleep.

At the first streak of dawn he was up, and
within a short half-mile, thanks to the snowy
mare, he found the band. At his approach,
the shrill neigh of the Pacer bugled his
troop into a flying squad. But on the first
mesa they stopped, and faced about to see what
this persistent follower was, and what he wanted.
For a moment or so they stood against the sky
to gaze, and then deciding that he knew him as
well as he wished to, that black meteor flung his
mane on the wind, and led off at his tireless,
even swing, while the mares came streaming
after.

Away they went, circling now to the west,
and after several repetitions of this same play,
flying, following, and overtaking, and flying
again, they passed, near noon, the old Apache
look-out, Buffalo Bluff. And here, on watch,
was Jo. A long thin column of smoke told
Charley to come to camp, and with a flashing
pocket-mirror he made response.

Jo, freshly mounted, rode across, and again
took up the chase, and back came Charley to

camp to eat and rest, and then move on up stream.

All that day Jo followed, and managed, when it was needed, that the herd should keep the great circle, of which the wagon cut a small chord. At sundown he came to Verde Crossing, and there was Charley with a fresh horse and food, and Jo went on in the same calm, dogged way. All the evening he followed, and far into the night, for the wild herd was now getting somewhat used to the presence of the harmless strangers, and were more easily followed; moreover, they were tiring out with perpetual travelling. They were no longer in the good grass country, they were not grain-fed like the horses on their track, and above all, the slight but continuous nervous tension was surely telling. It spoiled their appetites, but made them very thirsty. They were allowed, and as far as possible encouraged, to drink deeply at every chance. The effect of large quantities of water on a running animal is well known ; it tends to stiffen the limbs and spoil the wind. Jo carefully guarded his own horse against such excess, and both he and his horse were fresh when they camped that night on the trail of the jaded mustangs.

At dawn he found them easily close at hand, and though they ran at first they did not go far before they dropped into a walk. The battle

seemed nearly won now, for the chief difficulty in the ' walk-down ' is to keep track of the herd the first two or three days when they are fresh.

All that morning Jo kept in sight, generally in close sight, of the band. About ten o'clock, Charley relieved him near José Peak and that day the mustangs walked only a quarter of a mile ahead with much less spirit than the day before and circled now more north again. At night Charley was supplied with a fresh horse and followed as before.

Next day the mustangs walked with heads held low, and in spite of the efforts of the Black Pacer at times they were less than a hundred yards ahead of their pursuer.

The fourth and fifth days passed the same way, and now the herd was nearly back to Antelope Springs. So far all had come out as expected. The chase had been in a great circle

The Pacing Mustang

with the wagon following a lesser circle. The wild herd was back to its starting-point, worn out; and the hunters were back, fresh and on fresh horses. The herd was kept from drinking till late in the afternoon and then driven to the Springs to swell themselves with a perfect water gorge. Now was the chance for the skilful ropers on the grain-fed horses to close in, for the sudden heavy drink was ruination, almost paralysis, of wind and limb, and it would be easy to rope and hobble them one by one.

There was only one weak spot in the programme, the Black Stallion, the cause of the hunt, seemed made of iron, that ceaseless swinging pace seemed as swift and vigorous now as on the morning when the chase began. Up and down he went rounding up the herd and urging them on by voice and example to escape. But they were played out. The old white mare that had been such help in sighting them at night, had dropped out hours ago, dead beat. The half-bloods seemed to be losing all fear of the horsemen, the band was clearly in Jo's power. But the one who was the prize of all the hunt seemed just as far as ever out of reach.

Here was a puzzle. Jo's comrades knew
him well and would not have been surprised to
see him in a sudden rage attempt to shoot the
Stallion down. But Jo had no such mind.
During that long week of following he had
watched the horse all day at speed and never
once had he seen him gallop.

The horseman's adoration of a noble horse
had grown and grown, till now he would as
soon have thought of shooting his best mount
as firing on that splendid beast.

Jo even asked himself whether he would take
the handsome sum that was offered for the
prize. Such an animal would be a fortune in
himself to sire a race of pacers for the track.

But the prize was still at large—the time had
come to finish up the hunt. Jo's finest mount
was caught. She was a mare of Eastern blood,
but raised on the plains. She never would have
come into Jo's possession but for a curious weakness. The loco is a poisonous weed that grows
in these regions. Most stock will not touch it ;
but sometimes an animal tries it and becomes
addicted to it. It acts somewhat like morphine,
but the animal, though sane for long intervals,

LOCO-WEED

200

has always a passion for the herb and finally dies mad.. A beast with the craze is said to be locoed. And Jo's best mount had a wild gleam in her eye that to an expert told the tale.

But she was swift and strong and Jo chose her for the grand finish of the chase. It would have been an easy matter now to rope the mares, but was no longer necessary. They could be separated from their black leader and driven home to the corral. But that leader still had the look of untamed strength. Jo, rejoicing in a worthy foe, went bounding forth to try the odds. The lasso was flung on the ground and trailed to take out every kink, and gathered as he rode into neatest coils across his left palm. Then putting on the spur the first time in that chase he rode straight for the Stallion a quarter of a mile beyond. Away he went, and away went Jo, each at his best, while the fagged-out mares scattered right and left and let them pass. Straight across the open plain the fresh horse went at its hardest gallop, and the Stallion, leading off, still kept his start and kept his famous swing.

The Pacing Mustang

It was incredible, and Jo put on more spur and shouted to his horse, which fairly flew, but shortened up the space between by not a single inch. For the Black One whirled across the flat and up and passed a soapweed mesa and down across a sandy treacherous plain, then over a grassy stretch where prairie dogs barked, then hid below, and on came Jo, but there to see, could he believe his eyes, the Stallion's start grown longer still, and Jo began to curse his luck, and urge and spur his horse until the poor uncertain brute got into such a state of nervous fright, her eyes began to roll, she wildly shook her head from side to side, no longer picked her ground—a badger-hole received her foot and down she went, and Jo went flying to the earth. Though badly bruised, he gained his feet and tried to mount his crazy beast. But she, poor brute, was done for—her off fore-leg hung loose.

There was but one thing to do. Jo loosed the cinch, put Lightfoot out of pain, and carried back the saddle to the camp. While the Pacer steamed away till lost to view.

This was not quite defeat, for all the mares

were manageable now, and Jo and Charley drove them carefully to the 'L cross F' corral and claimed a good reward. But Jo was more than ever bound to own the Stallion. He had seen what stuff he was made of, he prized him more and more, and only sought to strike some better plan to catch him.

IV

The cook on that trip was Bates—Mr. Thomas Bates, he called himself at the post-office where he regularly went for the letters and remittance which never came. Old Tom Turkeytrack, the boys called him, from his cattle-brand, which he said was on record at Denver, and which, according to his story, was also borne by countless beef and saddle stock on the plains of the unknown North.

When asked to join the trip as a partner, Bates made some sarcastic remarks about horses not fetching $12 a dozen, which had been literally true within the year, and he preferred to go on a very meagre salary. But no one who once saw the Pacer going had failed to catch the craze.

Turkeytrack experienced the usual change of heart. He now wanted to own that mustang. How this was to be brought about he did not clearly see till one day there called at the ranch that had 'secured his services,' as he put it, one, Bill Smith, more usually known as Horseshoe Billy, from his cattle-brand. While the excellent fresh beef and bread and the vile coffee, dried peaches and molasses were being consumed, he of the horseshoe remarked, in tones which percolated through a huge stop-gap of bread :

" Wall, I seen that thar Pacer to-day, nigh enough to put a plait in his tail."

" What, you didn't shoot?"

" No, but I come mighty near it."

" Don't you be led into no sich foolishness," said a 'double-bar H' cow-puncher at the other end of the table. " I calc'late that maverick 'ill carry my brand before the moon changes."

" You'll have to be pretty spry or you'll find a ' triangle dot' on his weather side when you get there."

" Where did you run acrost him? "

" Wall, it was like this; I was riding the

The Pacing Mustang

flat by Antelope Springs and I sees a lump on the dry mud inside the rush belt. I knowed I never seen that before, so rides up, thinking it might be some of our stock, an' seen it was a horse lying plumb flat. The wind was blowing like —— from him to me, so I rides up close and seen it was the Pacer, dead as a mackerel. Still, he didn't look swelled or cut, and there wa'n't no smell, an' I didn't know what to think till I seen his ear twitch off a fly and then I knowed he was sleeping. I gits down me rope and coils it, and seen it was old and pretty shaky in spots, and me saddle a single cinch, an' me pony about 700 again a 1,200 lbs. stallion, an' I sez to meself, sez I: ''Tain't no use, I'll only break me cinch and git throwed an' lose me saddle.' So I hits the saddle-horn a crack with the hondu, and I wish't you'd a seen that mustang. He lept six foot in the air an' landed on all fours and snorted like he was shunting cars. His eyes fairly bugged out an' he lighted out lickety split for California, and he orter be there about now if he kep' on like he started—and I swear he never made a break the hull trip.''

The Pacing Mustang

The story was not quite so consecutive as given here. It was much punctuated by present engrossments, and from first to last was more or less infiltrated through the necessaries of life, for Bill was a healthy young man without a trace of false shame. But the account was complete and everyone believed it, for Billy was known to be reliable. Of all those who heard, old Turkeytrack talked the least and probably thought the most, for it gave him a new idea.

During his after-dinner pipe he studied it out and deciding that he could not go it alone, he took Horseshoe Billy into his council and the result was a partnership in a new venture to capture the Pacer; that is, the $5,000 that was now said to be the offer for him safe in a box-car.

Antelope Springs was still the usual watering-place of the Pacer. The water being low left a broad belt of dry black mud between the sedge and the spring. At two places this belt was broken by a well-marked trail made by the animals coming to drink. Horses and wild animals usually kept to these trails, though the horned cattle had no hesitation in taking a short cut through the sedge.

The Pacing Mustang

In the most used of these trails the two men set to work with shovels and digged a pit 15 feet long, 6 feet wide and 7 feet deep. It was a hard twenty hours work for them as it had to be completed between the Mustang's drinks, and it began to be very damp work before it was finished. With poles, brush, and earth it was then cleverly covered over and concealed. And the men went to a distance and hid in pits made for the purpose.

About noon the Pacer came, alone now since the capture of his band. The trail on the opposite side of the mud belt was little used, and old Tom, by throwing some fresh rushes across it, expected to make sure that the Stallion would enter by the other, if indeed he should by any caprice try to come by the unusual path.

What sleepless angel is it watches over and cares for the wild animals? In spite of all reasons to take the usual path, the Pacer came along the other. The suspicious-looking rushes did not stop him; he walked calmly to the water and drank. There was only one way now to prevent utter failure; when he lowered his head for the second draft which horses always take, Bates and Smith quit their holes and ran swiftly toward the trail behind him, and when he raised his proud head Smith sent a revolver-shot into the ground behind him.

Away went the Pacer at his famous gait straight to the trap. Another second and he would be into it. Already he is on the trail, and already they feel they have him, but the Angel of the wild things is with him, that incomprehensible warning comes, and with one mighty bound he clears the fifteen feet of treacherous ground and spurns the earth as he fades away unharmed, never again to visit Antelope Springs by either of the beaten paths.

V

Wild Jo never lacked energy. He meant to catch that Mustang, and when he learned that others were bestirring themselves for the same purpose he at once set about trying the best untried plan he knew—the plan by which the coyote catches the fleeter jackrabbit, and the mounted Indian the far swifter antelope—the old plan of the relay chase.

The Pacing Mustang

The Canadian River on the south, its affluent,
the Piñavetitos Arroyo, on the northeast, and
the Don Carlos Hills with the Ute Creek Cañon
on the west, formed a sixty-mile triangle that
was the range of the Pacer. It was believed
that he never went outside this, and at all times
Antelope Springs was his headquarters. Jo
knew this country well, all the water-holes
and cañon crossings as well as the ways of the
Pacer.

If he could have gotten fifty good horses he
could have posted them to advantage so as to
cover all points, but twenty mounts and five
good riders were all that proved available.

The horses, grain-fed for two weeks before,
were sent on ahead ; each man was instructed
now to play his part and sent to his post the day
before the race. On the day of the start Jo
with his wagon drove to the plain of Antelope
Springs and, camping far off in a little draw,
waited.

At last he came, that coal-black Horse, out
from the sand-hills at the south, alone as always
now, and walked calmly down to the Springs
and circled quite around it to sniff for any hid-

den foe.   Then he approached where there was
no trail at all and drank.

Jo watched and wished he would drink a
hogshead.   But the moment that he turned
and sought the grass Jo spurred his steed.   The
Pacer heard the hoofs, then saw the running
horse, and did not want a nearer view but led
away.   Across the flat he went down to the
south, and kept the famous swinging gait that
made his start grow longer.   Now through the
sandy dunes he went, and steadying to an even
pace he gained considerably and Jo's too-laden
horse plunged through the sand and sinking fet-
lock deep, lost at every bound.   Then came a level
stretch where the runner seemed to gain, and
then a long decline where Jo's horse dared not
run his best, so lost again at every step.

But on they went, and Jo spared neither spur
nor quirt.   A mile—a mile—and another mile,
and the far - off rock at Arriba loomed up
ahead.

And there Jo knew fresh mounts were held,
and on they dashed.   But the night-black
mane out level on the breeze ahead was gaining
more and more.

The Pacing Mustang

Arriba Cañon reached at last, the watcher stood aside, for it was not wished to turn the race, and the Stallion passed—dashed down, across and up the slope, with that unbroken pace, the only one he knew.

And Jo came bounding on his foaming steed, and leaped on the waiting mount, then urged him down the slope and up upon the track, and on the upland once more drove in the spurs, and raced and raced, and raced, but not a single inch he gained.

Ga-lump, ga-lump, ga-lump with measured beat he went—an hour—an hour, and another hour—Arroyo Alamosa just ahead with fresh relays, and Jo yelled at his horse and pushed him on and on. Straight for the place the Black One made, but on the last two miles some strange foreboding turned him to the left, and Jo foresaw escape in this, and pushed his jaded mount at any cost to head him off, and hard as they had raced this was the hardest race of all, with gasps for breath and leather squeaks at every straining bound. Then cutting right across, Jo seemed to gain, and drawing his gun he fired shot after shot to toss the dust, and so turned the Stallion's head and forced him back to take the crossing to the right.

Down they went. The Stallion crossed and Jo sprang to the ground. His horse was done, for thirty miles had passed in the last stretch, and Jo himself was worn out. His eyes were burnt with flying alkali dust. He was half blind so he motioned to his 'pard' to "go ahead and keep him straight for Alamosa ford."

Out shot the rider on a strong, fresh steed, and away they went—up and down on the rolling plain—the Black Horse flecked with snowy foam. His heaving ribs and noisy breath showed what he felt—but on and on he went.

And Tom on Ginger seemed to gain, then lose and lose, when in an hour the long decline of Alamosa came. And there a freshly mounted lad took up the chase and turned it west, and on they went past towns of prairie dogs, through soapweed tracts and cactus brakes by scores, and pricked and wrenched rode on. With dust and sweat the Black was now a dappled brown, but still he stepped the same. Young Carrington, who followed, had hurt his steed by pushing at the very start, and spurred

212

and urged him now to cut across a gulch at which the Pacer shied. Just one misstep and down they went.

The boy escaped, but the pony lies there yet, and the wild Black Horse kept on.

This was close to old Gallego's ranch where Jo himself had cut across refreshed to push the chase. Within thirty minutes he was again scorching the Pacer's trail.

Far in the west the Carlos Hills were seen, and there Jo knew fresh men and mounts were waiting, and that way the indomitable rider tried to turn the race, but by a sudden whim, of the inner warning born perhaps—the Pacer turned. Sharp to the north he went, and Jo, the skilful wrangler, rode and rode and yelled and tossed the dust with shots, but down a gulch the wild black meteor streamed and Jo could only follow. Then came the hardest race of all; Jo, cruel to the Mustang, was crueller to his mount and to himself. The sun was hot, the scorching plain was dim in shimmering heat, his eyes and lips were burnt with sand and salt, and yet the chase sped on. The only chance to win would be if he could drive the Mustang

back to Big Arroyo Crossing. Now almost for
the first time he saw signs of weakening in the
Black. His mane and tail were not just quite so
high, and his short half mile of start was down
by more than half, but still he stayed ahead
and paced and paced and paced.

An hour and another hour, and still they went
the same. But they turned again, and night
was near when big Arroyo ford was reached—
fully twenty miles. But Jo was game, he seized
the waiting horse. The one he left went gasping to the stream and gorged himself with water till he died.

Then Jo held back in hopes the foaming
Black would drink. But he was wise ; he gulped
a single gulp, splashed through the stream and
then passed on with Jo at speed behind him.
And when they last were seen the Black was on
ahead just out of reach and Jo's horse bounding on.

It was morning when Jo came to camp on
foot. His tale was briefly told :—eight horses
dead—five men worn out—the matchless Pacer
safe and free.

" 'Taint possible; it can't be done. Sorry I

didn't bore his hellish carcass through when I had the chance," said Jo, and gave it up.

VI

Old Turkeytrack was cook on this trip. He had watched the chase with as much interest as anyone, and when it failed he grinned into the pot and said: "That mustang's mine unless I'm a darned fool." Then falling back on Scripture for a precedent, as was his habit, he still addressed the pot:

"Reckon the Philistines tried to run Samson down and they got done up, an' would a stayed done ony for a nat'ral weakness on his part. An' Adam would a loafed in Eden yit ony for a leetle failing which we all onderstand. An' it aint $5000 I'll take for him nuther."

Much persecution had made the Pacer wilder than ever. But it did not drive him away from Antelope Springs. That was the only drinking-place with absolutely no shelter for a mile on every side to hide an enemy. Here he came

almost every day about noon, and after thoroughly spying the land approached to drink.

His had been a lonely life all winter since the capture of his harem, and of this old Turkeytrack was fully aware. The old cook's chum had a nice little brown mare which he judged would serve his ends, and taking a pair of the strongest hobbles, a spade, a spare lasso, and a stout post he mounted the mare and rode away to the famous Springs.

A few antelope skimmed over the plain before him in the early freshness of the day. Cattle were lying about in groups, and the loud, sweet song of the prairie lark was heard on every side. For the bright snowless winter of the mesas was gone and the springtime was at hand. The grass was greening and all nature seemed turning to thoughts of love.

It was in the air, and when the little brown mare was picketed out to graze she raised her nose from time to time to pour forth a long shrill whinny that surely was her song, if song she had, of love.

Old Turkeytrack studied the wind and the lay of the land. There was the pit he had labored at, now opened and filled with water that

was rank with drowned prairie dogs and mice.
Here was the new trail the animals were forced
to make by the pit. He selected a sedgy clump
near some smooth, grassy ground, and first
firmly sunk the post, then dug a hole large
enough to hide in, and spread his blanket in it.
He shortened up the little mare's tether, till she
could scarcely move; then on the ground between he spread his open lasso, tying the long
end to the post, then covered the rope with
dust and grass, and went into his hiding-place.

About noon, after long waiting, the amorous
whinny of the mare was answered from the high
ground, away to the west, and there, black
against the sky, was the famous Mustang.

Down he came at that long swinging gait,
but grown crafty with much pursuit, he often
stopped to gaze and whinny, and got answer
that surely touched his heart. Nearer he came
again to call, then took alarm, and paced all
around in a great circle to try the wind for his
foes, and seemed in doubt. The Angel whispered "Don't go." But the brown mare called
again. He circled nearer still, and neighed
once more, and got reply that seemed to quell
all fears, and set his heart aglow.

The Pacing Mustang

Nearer still he pranced, till he touched Solly's nose with his own, and finding her as responsive as he well could wish, thrust aside all thoughts of danger, and abandoned himself to the delight of conquest, until, as he pranced around, his hind legs for a moment stood within the evil circle of the rope. One deft sharp twitch, the noose flew tight, and he was caught.

A snort of terror and a bound in the air gave Tom the chance to add the double hitch. The loop flashed up the line, and snake-like bound those mighty hoofs.

Terror lent speed and double strength for a moment, but the end of the rope was reached, and down he went a captive, a hopeless prisoner at last. Old Tom's ugly, little crooked form sprang from the pit to complete the mastering of the great glorious creature whose mighty strength had proved as nothing when matched with the wits of a little old man. With snorts and desperate bounds of awful force the great beast dashed and struggled to be free; but all in vain. The rope was strong.

The second lasso was deftly swung, and the forefeet caught, and then with a skilful move

The Pacing Mustang

the feet were drawn together, and down went
the raging Pacer to lie a moment later 'hog-tied'
and helpless on the ground.   There he struggled
till worn out, sobbing great convulsive sobs
while tears ran down his cheeks.

Tom stood by and watched, but a strange re-
vulsion of feeling came over the old cow-
puncher.   He trembled nervously from head to
foot, as he had not done since he roped his first
steer, and for a while could do nothing but gaze
on his tremendous prisoner. But the feeling soon
passed away.   He saddled Delilah, and taking
the second lasso, roped the great horse about
the neck, and left the mare to hold the Stallion's
head, while he put on the hobbles.   This was
soon done, and sure of him now old Bates was
about to loose the ropes, but on a sudden
thought he stopped.   He had quite forgotten,
and had come unprepared for something of importance.   In Western law the Mustang was the
property of the first man to mark him with his
brand ; how was this to be done with the nearest branding-iron twenty miles away ?

Old Tom went to his mare, took up her hoofs
one at a time, and examined each shoe.   Yes !

one was a little loose; he pushed and pried it
with the spade, and got it off. Buffalo chips
and kindred fuel were plentiful about the plain,
so a fire was quickly made, and he soon had one
arm of the horse-shoe red hot, then holding the
other wrapped in his sock he rudely sketched

on the left shoulder of the helpless mustang a
turkeytrack, his brand, the first time really
that it had ever been used. The Pacer shud-
dered as the hot iron seared his flesh, but it was
quickly done, and the famous Mustang Stallion
was a maverick no more.

Now all there was to do was to take him
home. The ropes were loosed, the Mustang
felt himself freed, thought he was free, and
sprang to his feet only to fall as soon as he
tried to take a stride. His forefeet were strongly tied together, his only possible gait a shuf-
fling walk, or else a desperate labored bounding
with feet so unnaturally held that within a few
yards he was inevitably thrown each time he
tried to break away. Tom on the light pony
headed him off again and again, and by dint of
driving, threatening, and manœuvring, contrived to force his foaming, crazy captive north-

The Pacing Mustang

ward toward the Piñavetitos Cañon. But the wild horse would not drive, would not give in. With snorts of terror or of rage and maddest bounds, he tried and tried to get away. It was one long cruel fight; his glossy sides were thick with dark foam, and the foam was stained with blood. Countless hard falls and exhaustion that a long day's chase was powerless to produce were telling on him; his straining bounds first this way and then that, were not now quite so strong, and the spray he snorted as he gasped was half a spray of blood. But his captor, relentless, masterful and cool, still forced him on. Down the slope toward the cañon they had come, every yard a fight, and now they were at the head of the draw that took the trail down to the only crossing of the cañon, the northmost limit of the Pacer's ancient range.

From this the first corral and ranch-house were in sight. The man rejoiced, but the Mustang gathered his remaining strength for one more desperate dash. Up, up the grassy slope from the trail he went, defied the swinging, slashing rope and the gunshot fired in air, in vain attempt to turn his frenzied course.

The Pacing Mustang

Up, up and on, above the sheerest cliff he dashed
then sprang away into the vacant air, down—
down—two hundred downward feet to fall, and
land upon the rocks below, a lifeless wreck—
but free.

Wully
The Story of a Yaller Dog

Wully

The Story of a Yaller Dog

WULLY was a little yaller dog. A yaller dog, be it understood, is not necessarily the same as a yellow dog. He is not simply a canine whose capillary covering is highly charged with yellow pigment. He is the mongrelest mixture of all mongrels, the least common multiple of all dogs, the breedless union of all breeds, and though of no breed at all, he is yet of older, better breed than any of his aristocratic relations, for he is nature's attempt to restore the ancestral jackal, the parent stock of all dogs.

Indeed, the scientific name of the jackal (*Canis aureus*) means simply 'yellow dog,' and not a few of that animal's characteristics are seen in his domesticated representative. For the plebeian cur is shrewd, active, and hardy, and

Wully

far better equipped for the real struggle of life than any of his 'thoroughbred' kinsmen.

If we were to abandon a yaller dog, a greyhound, and a bulldog on a desert island, which of them after six months would be alive and well? Unquestionably it would be the despised yellow cur. He has not the speed of the greyhound, but neither does he bear the seeds of lung and skin diseases. He has not the strength or reckless courage of the bulldog, but he has something a thousand times better, he has *common sense.* Health and wit are no mean equipment for the life struggle, and when the dog-world is not 'managed' by man, they have never yet failed to bring out the yellow mongrel as the sole and triumphant survivor.

Once in a while the reversion to the jackal type is more complete, and the yaller dog has pricked and pointed ears. Beware of him then. He is cunning and plucky and can bite like a wolf. There is a strange, wild streak in his nature too, that under cruelty or long adversity may develop into deadliest treachery in spite of the better traits that are the foundation of man's love for the dog.

226

Wully

I

WAY up in the Cheviots little Wully was born. He and one other of the litter were kept; his brother because he resembled the best dog in the vicinity, and himself because he was a little yellow beauty.

His early life was that of a sheep-dog, in company with an experienced collie who trained him, and an old shepherd who was scarcely inferior to them in intelligence. By the time he was two years old Wully was full grown and had taken a thorough course in sheep. He knew them from ram-horn to lamb-hoof, and old Robin, his master, at length had such confidence in his sagacity that he would frequently stay at the tavern all night while Wully guarded the woolly idiots in the hills. His education had been wisely bestowed and in most ways he was a very bright little dog with a future before him. Yet he never learned to despise that addle-pated Robin. The old shepherd, with all his faults, his continual

227

striving after his ideal state—intoxication—and his mind-shrivelling life in general was rarely brutal to Wully, and Wully repaid him with an exaggerated worship that the greatest and wisest in the land would have aspired to in vain.

Wully could not have imagined any greater being than Robin, and yet for the sum of five shillings a week all Robin's vital energy and mental force were pledged to the service of a not very great cattle and sheep dealer, the real proprietor of Wully's charge, and when this man, really less great than the neighboring laird, ordered Robin to drive his flock by stages to the Yorkshire moors and markets, of all the 376 mentalities concerned, Wully's was the most interested and interesting.

The journey through Northumberland was uneventful. At the River Tyne the sheep were driven on to the ferry and landed safely in smoky South Shields. The great factory chimneys were just starting up for the day and belching out fogbanks and thunder-rollers of opaque leaden smoke that darkened the air and hung low like a storm-cloud over the streets. The sheep thought that they recognized the fuming

dun of an unusually heavy Cheviot storm. They became alarmed, and in spite of their keepers stampeded through the town in 374 different directions.

Robin was vexed to the inmost recesses of his tiny soul. He stared stupidly after the sheep for half a minute, then gave the order, "Wully, fetch them in." After this mental effort he sat down, lit his pipe, and taking out his knitting began work on a half-finished sock.

To Wully the voice of Robin was the voice of God. Away he ran in 374 different directions, and headed off and rounded up the 374 different wanderers, and brought them back to the ferry-house before Robin, who was stolidly watching the process, had toed off his sock.

Finally Wully—not Robin—gave the sign that all were in. The old shepherd proceeded to count them—370, 371, 372, 373.

"Wully," he said reproachfully, "thar no' a' here. Thur's anither." And Wully, stung with shame, bounded off to scour the whole city for the missing one. He was not long gone when a small boy pointed out to Robin that the sheep were all there, the whole 374. Now Robin was in a quandary. His order was to hasten on to Yorkshire, and yet he knew that Wully's pride would prevent his coming back without another sheep, even if he had to steal it. Such things had happened before, and resulted in embarrassing complications. What should he do? There was five shillings a week at stake. Wully was a good dog, it was a pity to lose him, but then, his orders from the master; and again, if Wully stole an extra sheep to make up the number, then what—in a foreign land too? He decided to abandon Wully, and push on alone with the sheep. And how he fared no one knows or cares.

Meanwhile, Wully careered through miles of streets hunting in vain for his lost sheep. All day he searched, and at night, famished and worn out, he sneaked shamefacedly back to the ferry, only to find that master and sheep had gone. His sorrow was pitiful to see. He ran about whimpering, then took the ferryboat across to the other side, and searched everywhere for Robin. He returned to South Shields and searched there, and spent the rest

Wully

of the night seeking for his wretched idol. The next day he continued his search, he crossed and recrossed the river many times. He watched and smelt everyone that came over, and with significant shrewdness he sought unceasingly in the neighboring taverns for his master. The next day he set to work systematically to smell everyone that might cross the ferry.

The ferry makes fifty trips a day, with an average of one hundred persons a trip, yet never once did Wully fail to be on the gang-plank and smell every pair of legs that crossed—5,000 pairs, 10,000 legs that day did Wully examine after his own fashion. And the next day, and the next, and all the week he kept his post, and seemed indifferent to feeding himself. Soon starvation and worry began to tell on him. He grew thin and ill-tempered. No one could touch him, and any attempt to interfere with his daily occupation of leg-smelling roused him to desperation.

Day after day, week after week Wully watched and waited for his master, who never came. The ferry men learned to respect

231

Wully's fidelity. At first he scorned their proffered food and shelter, and lived no one knew how, but starved to it at last, he accepted the gifts and learned to tolerate the givers. Although embittered against the world, his heart was true to his worthless master.

Fourteen months afterward I made his acquaintance. He was still on rigid duty at his post. He had regained his good looks. His bright, keen face set off by his white ruff and pricked ears made a dog to catch the eye anywhere. But he gave me no second glance, once he found my legs were not those he sought, and in spite of my friendly overtures during the ten months following that he continued his watch, I got no farther into his confidence than any other stranger.

For two whole years did this devoted creature attend that ferry. There was only one thing to prevent him going home to the hills, not the distance nor the chance of getting lost, but the conviction that Robin, the godlike Robin, wished him to stay by the ferry; and he stayed.

But he crossed the water as often as he felt

it would serve his purpose. The fare for a dog was one penny, and it was calculated that Wully owed the company hundreds of pounds before he gave up his quest. He never failed to sense every pair of nethers that crossed the gangplank — 6,000,000 legs by computation had been pronounced upon by this expert. But all to no purpose. His unswerving fidelity never faltered, though his temper was obviously souring under the long strain.

We had never heard what became of Robin, but one day a sturdy drover strode down the ferry-slip and Wully mechanically assaying the new personality, suddenly started, his mane bristled, he trembled, a low growl escaped him, and he fixed his every sense on the drover.

One of the ferry hands not understanding, called to the stranger, " Hoot mon, ye maunna hort oor dawg."

" Whaes hortin 'im, ye fule ; he is mair like to hort me." But further explanation was not necessary. Wully's manner had wholly changed. He fawned on the drover, and his tail was wagging violently for the first time in years.

Wully

A few words made it all clear. Dorley, the drover, had known Robin very well, and the mittens and comforter he wore were of Robin's own make and had once been part of his wardrobe. Wully recognized the traces of his master, and despairing of any nearer approach to his lost idol, he abandoned his post at the ferry and plainly announced his intention of sticking to the owner of the mittens, and Dorley was well-pleased to take Wully along to his home among the hills of Derbyshire, where he became once more a sheep-dog in charge of a flock.

II

Monsaldale is one of the best-known valleys in Derbyshire. The Pig and Whistle is its single but celebrated inn, and Jo Greatorex, the landlord, is a shrewd and sturdy Yorkshireman. Nature meant him for a frontiersman, but circumstances made him an innkeeper and his inborn tastes made him a—well, never mind; there was a great deal of poaching done in that country.

Wully's new home was on the upland east of

234

the valley above Jo's inn, and that fact was not without weight in bringing me to Monsaldale. His master, Dorley, farmed in a small way on the lowland, and on the moors had a large number of sheep. These Wully guarded with his old-time sagacity, watching them while they fed and bringing them to the fold at night. He was reserved and preoccupied for a dog, and rather too ready to show his teeth to strangers, but he was so unremitting in his attention to his flock that Dorley did not lose a lamb that year, although the neighboring farmers paid the usual tribute to eagles and to foxes.

The dales are poor fox-hunting country at best. The rocky ridges, high stone walls, and precipices are too numerous to please the riders, and the final retreats in the rocks are so plentiful that it was a marvel the foxes did not overrun Monsaldale. But they didn't. There had been but little reason for complaint until the year 1881, when a sly old fox quartered himself on the fat parish, like a mouse inside a cheese, and laughed equally at the hounds of the huntsmen and the lurchers of the farmers.

He was several times run by the Peak hounds,

and escaped by making for the Devil's Hole.
Once in this gorge, where the cracks in the
rocks extend unknown distances, he was safe.
The country folk began to see something more
than chance in the fact that he always escaped
at the Devil's Hole, and when one of the
hounds who nearly caught this Devil's Fox
soon after went mad, it removed all doubt as
to the spiritual paternity of said fox.

He continued his career of rapine, making
audacious raids and hair-breadth escapes, and
finally began, as do many old foxes, to kill from
a mania for slaughter. Thus it was that Digby
lost ten lambs in one night. Carroll lost seven
the next night. Later, the vicarage duck-pond
was wholly devastated, and scarcely a night
passed but someone in the region had to report
a carnage of poultry, lambs or sheep, and, finally
even calves.

Of course all the slaughter was attributed to
this one fox of the Devil's Hole. It was known
only that he was a very large fox, at least one
that made a very large track. He never was
clearly seen, even by the huntsmen. And it
was noticed that Thunder and Bell, the stanch-

236

est hounds in the pack, had refused to tongue or even to follow the trail when he was hunted.

His reputation for madness sufficed to make the master of the Peak hounds avoid the neighborhood. The farmers in Monsaldale, led by Jo, agreed among themselves that if it would only come on a snow, they would assemble and beat the whole country, and in defiance of all rules of the hunt, get rid of the ' daft ' fox in any way they could. But the snow did not come, and the red-haired gentleman lived his life. Notwithstanding his madness, he did not lack method. He never came two successive nights to the same farm. He never ate where he killed, and he never left a track that betrayed his retreat. He usually finished up his night's trail on the turf, or on a public highway.

Once I saw him. I was walking to Monsaldale from Bakewell late one night during a heavy storm, and as I turned the corner of Stead's sheep-fold there was a vivid flash of lightning. By its light, there was fixed on my retina a picture that made me start. Sitting on his haunches by the roadside, twenty yards away, was a very large fox gazing at me with

237

malignant eyes, and licking his muzzle in a suggestive manner. All this I saw, but no more, and might have forgotten it, or thought myself mistaken, but the next morning, in that very fold, were found the bodies of twenty-three lambs and sheep, and the unmistakable signs that brought home the crime to the well-known marauder.

There was only one man who escaped, and that was Dorley. This was the more remarkable because he lived in the centre of the region raided, and within one mile of the Devil's Hole. Faithful Wully proved himself worth all the dogs in the neighborhood. Night after night he brought in the sheep, and never one was missing. The Mad Fox might prowl about the Dorley homestead if he wished, but Wully, shrewd, brave, active Wully was more than a match for him, and not only saved his master's flock, but himself escaped with a whole skin. Everyone entertained a profound respect for him, and he might have been a popular pet but for his temper which, never genial, became more and more crabbed. He seemed to like Dorley, and Huldah, Dorley's eldest daughter,

Wully

a shrewd, handsome, young woman, who, in the capacity of general manager of the house, was Wully's special guardian. The other members of Dorley's family Wully learned to tolerate, but the rest of the world, men and dogs, he seemed to hate.

His uncanny disposition was well shown in the last meeting I had with him. I was walking on a pathway across the moor behind Dorley's house. Wully was lying on the doorstep. As I drew near he arose, and without appearing to see me trotted toward my pathway and placed himself across it about ten yards ahead of me. There he stood silently and intently regarding the distant moor, his slightly bristling mane the only sign that he had not been suddenly turned to stone. He did not stir as I came up, and not wishing to quarrel, I stepped around past his nose and walked on. Wully at once left his position and in the same eerie silence trotted on some twenty feet and again stood across the pathway. Once more I came up and, stepping into the grass, brushed past his nose. Instantly, but without a sound, he seized my left heel, I kicked out with the other foot,

but he escaped. Not having a stick, I flung a large stone at him. He leaped forward and the stone struck him in the ham, bowling him over into a ditch. He gasped out a savage growl as he fell, but scrambled out of the ditch and limped away in silence.

Yet sullen and ferocious as Wully was to the world, he was always gentle with Dorley's sheep. Many were the tales of rescues told of him. Many a poor lamb that had fallen into a pond or hole would have perished but for his timely and sagacious aid, many a far-weltered ewe did he turn right side up ; while his keen eye discerned and his fierce courage baffled every eagle that had appeared on the moor in his time.

III

The Monsaldale farmers were still paying their nightly tribute to the Mad Fox, when the snow came, late in December. Poor Widow Gelt lost her entire flock of twenty sheep, and the fiery cross went forth early in the morning. With guns unconcealed the burly farmers set out to follow to the finish the tell-tale tracks in

Wully

the snow, those of a very large fox, undoubtedly
the multo-murderous villain. For awhile the
trail was clear enough, then it came to the river
and the habitual cunning of the animal was
shown. He reached the water at a long angle
pointing down stream and jumped into the
shallow, unfrozen current. But at the other
side there was no track leading out, and it was
only after long searching that, a quarter of a
mile higher up the stream, they found where
he had come out. The track then ran to the
top of Henley's high stone wall, where there
was no snow left to tell tales. But the patient
hunters persevered. When it crossed the smooth
snow from the wall to the high road there was
a difference of opinion. Some claimed that the
track went up, others down the road. But Jo
settled it, and after another long search they
found where apparently the same trail, though
some said a larger one had left the road to enter
a sheep-fold, and leaving this without harming
the occupants, the track-maker had stepped in
the footmarks of a countryman, thereby getting
to the moor road, along which he had trotted
straight to Dorley's farm.

That day the sheep were kept in on account of the snow and Wully, without his usual occupation, was lying on some planks in the sun. As the hunters drew near the house, he growled savagely and sneaked around to where the sheep were. Jo Greatorex walked up to where Wully had crossed the fresh snow, gave a glance, looked dumbfounded, then pointing to the retreating sheep-dog, he said, with emphasis :

" Lads, we're off the track of the Fox. But there's the killer of the Widder's yowes."

Some agreed with Jo, others recalled the doubt in the trail and were for going back to make a fresh follow. At this juncture, Dorley himself came out of the house.

" Tom," said Jo, " that dog o' thine 'as killed twenty of Widder Gelt's sheep, last night. An' ah fur one don't believe as it is first killin'."

" Why, mon, thou art crazy," said Tom, " Ah never 'ad a better sheep-dog—'e fair loves the sheep."

" Aye ! We's seen summat o' that in las' night's work," replied Jo.

In vain the company related the history of

the morning. Tom swore that it was nothing but a jealous conspiracy to rob him of Wully.

"Wully sleeps i' the kitchen every night. Never is oot till he's let to bide wi' the yowes. Why, mon, he's wi' oor sheep the year round, and never a hoof have ah lost."

Tom became much excited over this abominable attempt against Wully's reputation and life. Jo and his partisans got equally angry, and it was a wise suggestion of Huldah's that quieted them.

"Feyther," said she, "ah'll sleep i' the kitchen the night. If Wully 'as ae way of gettin' oot ah'll see it, an' if he's no oot an' sheep's killed on the country-side, we'll ha' proof it's na Wully."

That night Huldah stretched herself on the settee and Wully slept as usual underneath the table. As night wore on the dog became restless. He turned on his bed and once or twice got up, stretched, looked at Huldah and lay down again. About two o'clock he seemed no longer able to resist some strange impulse. He arose quietly, looked toward the low window, then at the motionless girl. Huldah lay still and breathed as though sleeping. Wully slowly came near and sniffed and breathed his doggy breath in her face. She made no move. He nudged her gently with his nose. Then, with his sharp ears forward and his head on one side he studied her calm face. Still no sign. He walked quietly to the window, mounted the table without noise, placed his nose under the sash-bar and raised the light frame until he could put one paw underneath. Then changing, he put his nose under the sash and raised it high enough to slip out, easing down the frame finally on his rump and tail with an adroitness that told of long practice. Then he disappeared into the darkness.

From her couch Huldah watched in amazement. After waiting for some time to make sure that he was gone, she arose, intending to call her father at once, but on second thought she decided to await more conclusive proof. She peered into the darkness, but no sign of Wully was to be seen. She put more wood on the fire, and lay down again. For over an hour she lay wide awake listening to the kitchen clock, and starting at each trifling sound, and wondering what the dog was doing. Could it be possible that he had really killed the widow's sheep? Then the recollection of his gentleness to their own sheep came, and completed her perplexity.

Another hour slowly tick-tocked. She heard a slight sound at the window that made her heart jump. The scratching sound was soon followed by the lifting of the sash, and in a short time Wully was back in the kitchen with the window closed behind him.

By the flickering fire-light Huldah could see a strange, wild gleam in his eye, and his jaws and snowy breast were dashed with fresh blood. The dog ceased his slight panting as he scrutinized the girl. Then, as she did not move, he lay down, and began to lick his paws and muzzle, growling lowly once or twice as though at the remembrance of some recent occurrence.

Huldah had seen enough. There could no longer be any doubt that Jo was right and more —a new thought flashed into her quick brain, she realized that the weird fox of Monsal was before her. Raising herself, she looked straight at Wully, and exclaimed:

"Wully! Wully! so it's a' true—oh, Wully, ye terrible brute."

Her voice was fiercely reproachful, it rang in the quiet kitchen, and Wully recoiled as though shot. He gave a desperate glance toward the closed window. His eye gleamed, and his mane bristled. But he cowered under her gaze, and grovelled on the floor as though begging for mercy. Slowly he crawled nearer and nearer, as if to lick her feet, until quite close, then, with the fury of a tiger, but without a sound, he sprang for her throat.

The girl was taken unawares, but she threw up her arm in time, and Wully's long, gleaming tusks sank into her flesh, and grated on the bone.

"Help! help! feyther! feyther!" she shrieked.

Wully was a light weight, and for a moment she flung him off. But there could be no mistaking his purpose. The game was up, it was his life or hers now.

"Feyther! feyther!" she screamed, as the yellow fury, striving to kill her, bit and tore the unprotected hands that had so often fed him.

Wully

In vain she fought to hold him off, he would soon have had her by the throat, when in rushed Dorley.

Straight at him, now in the same horrid silence sprang Wully, and savagely tore him again and again before a deadly blow from the fagot-hook disabled him, dashing him, gasping and writhing, on the stone floor, desperate, and done for, but game and defiant to the last. Another quick blow scattered his brains on the hearth-stone, where so long he had been a faithful and honored retainer—and Wully, bright, fierce, trusty, treacherous Wully, quivered a moment, then straightened out, and lay forever still.

Redruff

The Story of the
Don Valley Partridge

Redruff

The Story of the Don Valley Partridge

I

OWN the wooded slope of Taylor's Hill the Mother Partridge led her brood; down toward the crystal brook that by some strange whim was called Mud Creek. Her little ones were one day old but already quick on foot, and she was taking them for the first time to drink.

She walked slowly, crouching low as she went, for the woods were full of enemies. She was uttering a soft little cluck in her throat, a call to the little balls of mottled down that on their tiny pink legs came toddling after, and peeping softly and plaintively if left even a few inches

behind, and seeming so fragile they made the
very chicadees look big and coarse. There
were twelve of them, but Mother Grouse
watched them all, and she watched every bush
and tree and thicket, and the whole woods and
the sky itself. Always for enemies she seemed
seeking—friends were too scarce to be looked
for—and an enemy she found. Away across
the level beaver meadow was a great brute of a
fox. He was coming their way, and in a few
moments would surely wind them or strike their
trail. There was no time to lose.

' *Krrr! Krrr!* ' (Hide! Hide!) cried the
mother in a low firm voice, and the little bits
of things, scarcely bigger than acorns and but a
day old, scattered far (a few inches) apart to
hide. One dived under a leaf, another between
two roots, a third crawled into a curl of birch-
bark, a fourth into a hole, and so on, till all
were hidden but one who could find no cover,
so squatted on a broad yellow chip and lay very
flat, and closed his eyes very tight, sure that
now he was safe from being seen. They ceased
their frightened peeping and all was still.

Mother Partridge flew straight toward the

252

dreaded beast, alighted fearlessly a few yards to one side of him, and then flung herself on the ground, flopping as though winged and lame—oh, so dreadfully lame—and whining like a distressed puppy. Was she begging for mercy—mercy from a bloodthirsty, cruel fox ? Oh, dear no ! She was no fool. One often hears of the cunning of the fox. Wait and see what a fool he is compared with a mother-partridge. Elated at the prize so suddenly within his reach, the fox turned with a dash and caught—at least, no, he didn't quite catch the bird ; she flopped by chance just a foot out of reach. He followed with another jump and would have seized her this time surely, but somehow a sapling came just between, and the partridge dragged herself awkwardly away and under a log, but the great brute snapped his jaws and bounded over the log, while she, seeming a trifle less lame, made another clumsy forward spring and tumbled down a bank, and Reynard, keenly following, almost caught her tail, but, oddly enough, fast as he went and leaped, she still seemed just a trifle faster. It was most extraordinary. A winged partridge and he, Reynard, the Swift-foot, had not caught her in five minutes' racing. It was really shameful. But the partridge seemed to gain strength as the fox put forth his, and after a quarter of a mile race, racing that was somehow all away from Taylor's Hill, the bird got unaccountably quite well, and, rising with a derisive whirr, flew off through the woods leaving the fox utterly dumfounded to realize that he had been made a fool of, and, worst of all, he now remembered that this was not the first time he had been served this very trick, though he never knew the reason for it.

Meanwhile Mother Partridge skimmed in a great circle and came by a roundabout way back to the little fuzz-balls she had left hidden in the woods.

With a wild bird's keen memory for places, she went to the very grass-blade she last trod on, and stood for a moment fondly to admire the perfect stillness of her children. Even at her step not one had stirred, and the little fellow on the chip, not so very badly concealed after all, had not budged, nor did he now; he only closed his eyes a tiny little bit harder, till the mother said:

Redruff

'*K-reet!*' (Come, children) and instantly like a fairy story, every hole gave up its little baby-partridge, and the wee fellow on the chip, the biggest of them all really, opened his big-little eyes and ran to the shelter of her broad tail, with a sweet little '*peep peep*' which an enemy could not have heard three feet away, but which his mother could not have missed thrice as far, and all the other thimblefuls of down joined in, and no doubt thought themselves dreadfully noisy, and were proportionately happy.

The sun was hot now. There was an open space to cross on the road to the water, and, after a careful lookout for enemies, the mother gathered the little things under the shadow of her spread fantail and kept off all danger of sunstroke until they reached the brier thicket by the stream.

Here a cottontail rabbit leaped out and gave them a great scare. But the flag of truce he carried behind was enough. He was an old friend ; and among other things the little ones learned that day that Bunny always sails under a flag of truce, and lives up to it too.

And then came the drink, the purest of living water, though silly men had called it Mud Creek.

At first the little fellows didn't know how to drink, but they copied their mother, and soon learned to drink like her and give thanks after every sip. There they stood in a row along the edge, twelve little brown and golden balls on twenty-four little pink-toed, in-turned feet, with twelve sweet little golden heads gravely bowing, drinking and giving thanks like their mother.

Then she led them by short stages, keeping the cover, to the far side of the beaver-meadow, where was a great grassy dome. The mother had made a note of this dome some time before. It takes a number of such domes to raise a brood of partridges. For this was an ant's nest. The old one stepped on top, looked about a moment, then gave half a dozen vigorous rakes with her claws. The friable ant-hill was broken open, and the earthen galleries scattered in ruins down the slope. The ants swarmed out and quarrelled with each other for lack of a better plan. Some ran around the hill with vast energy and little purpose, while a few of the more sensible began

to carry away fat white eggs. But the old partridge, coming to the little ones, picked up one
of these juicy-looking bags and clucked and
dropped it, and picked it up again and again
and clucked, then swallowed it. The young
ones stood around, then one little yellow fellow, the one that sat on the chip, picked up an
ant-egg, dropped it a few times, then yielding
to a sudden impulse, swallowed it, and so had
learned to eat. Within twenty minutes even
the runt had learned, and a merry time they had
scrambling after the delicious eggs as their
mother broke open more ant-galleries, and sent
them and their contents rolling down the bank,
till every little partridge had so crammed his
little crop that he was positively misshapen and
could eat no more.

Then all went cautiously up the stream, and
on a sandy bank, well screened by brambles, they
lay for all that afternoon, and learned how pleas-
ant it was to feel the cool powdery dust running
between their hot little toes. With their strong
bent for copying, they lay on their sides like
their mother and scratched with their tiny feet
and flopped with their wings, though they had

257

no wings to flop with, only a little tag among the down on each side, to show where the wings would come. That night she took them to a dry thicket near by, and there among the crisp, dead leaves that would prevent an enemy's silent approach on foot, and under the interlacing briers that kept off all foes of the air, she cradled them in their feather-shingled nursery and rejoiced in the fulness of a mother's joy over the wee cuddling things that peeped in their sleep and snuggled so trustfully against her warm body.

II

The third day the chicks were much stronger on their feet. They no longer had to go around an acorn ; they could even scramble over pine-cones, and on the little tags that marked the places for their wings, were now to be seen blue rows of fat blood-quills.

Their start in life was a good mother, good legs, a few reliable instincts, and a germ of reason. It was instinct, that is, inherited habit, which taught them to hide at the word from their mother; it was instinct that taught them to follow her, but it was reason which made them keep under the shadow of her tail when the sun was smiting down, and from that day reason entered more and more into their expanding lives.

Next day the blood-quills had sprouted the tips of feathers. On the next, the feathers were well out, and a week later the whole family of down-clad babies were strong on the wing.

And yet not all—poor little Runtie had been sickly from the first. He bore his half-shell on his back for hours after he came out; he ran less and cheeped more than his brothers, and when one evening at the onset of a skunk the mother gave the word '*Kwit, kwit*' (Fly, fly), Runtie was left behind, and when she gathered her brood on the piney hill he was missing, and they saw him no more.

Meanwhile, their training had gone on. They knew that the finest grasshoppers abounded in the long grass by the brook; they knew that the currant-bushes dropped fatness in the form of smooth, green worms; they knew that the dome of an ant-hill rising against the distant woods stood for a garner of plenty; they knew

that strawberries, though not really insects, were almost as delicious; they knew that the huge danaid butterflies were good, safe game, if they could only catch them, and that a slab of bark dropping from the side of a rotten log was sure to abound in good things of many different kinds; and they had learned, also, that yellow-jackets, mud-wasps, woolly worms, and hundred-leggers were better let alone.

It was now July, the Moon of Berries. The chicks had grown and flourished amazingly during this last month, and were now so large that in her efforts to cover them the mother was kept standing all night.

They took their daily dust-bath, but of late had changed to another higher on the hill. It was one in use by many different birds, and at first the mother disliked the idea of such a sec-ond-hand bath. But the dust was of such a fine, agreeable quality, and the children led the way with such enthusiasm, that she forgot her mis-trust.

After a fortnight the little ones began to droop and she herself did not feel very well. They were always hungry, and though they ate

Redruff

enormously, they one and all grew thinner and thinner. The mother was the last to be affected. But when it came, it came as hard on her—a ravenous hunger, a feverish headache, and a wasting weakness. She never knew the cause. She could not know that the dust of the much-used dust-bath, that her true instinct taught her to mistrust at first, and now again to shun, was sown with parasitic worms, and that all of the family were infested.

No natural impulse is without a purpose. The mother-bird's knowledge of healing was only to follow natural impulse. The eager, feverish craving for something, she knew not what, led her to eat, or try, everything that looked eatable and to seek the coolest woods. And there she found a deadly sumach laden with its poison· fruit. A month ago she would have passed it by, but now she tried the unattractive berries. The acrid burning juice seemed to answer some strange demand of her body; she ate and ate, and all her family joined in the strange feast of physic. No human doctor could have hit it better ; it proved a biting, drastic purge, the dreadful secret foe was downed, the danger

POISON
SUMAC

passed. But not for all — Nature, the old
nurse, had come too late for two of them. The
weakest, by inexorable law, dropped out. En-
feebled by the disease, the remedy was too se-
vere for them. They drank and drank by the
stream, and next morning did not move when
the others followed the mother. Strange vengeance was theirs now, for a skunk, the same
that could have told where Runtie went, found
and devoured their bodies and died of the poison they had eaten.

Seven little partridges now obeyed the
mother's call. Their individual characters
were early shown and now developed fast. The
weaklings were gone, but there were still a fool
and a lazy one. The mother could not help
caring for some more than for others, and her
favorite was the biggest, he who once sat on the
yellow chip for concealment. He was not only
the biggest, strongest, and handsomest of the
brood, but best of all, the most obedient. His
mother's warning ' *rrrrr* ' (danger) did not
always keep the others from a risky path or a
doubtful food, but obedience seemed natural to
him, and he never failed to respond to her soft

Redruff

' *K-reet*' (Come), and of this obedience he
reaped the reward, for his days were longest in
the land.

August, the Molting Moon, went by; the
young ones were now three parts grown. They
knew just enough to think themselves wonderfully wise. When they were small it was necessary to sleep on the ground so their mother
could shelter them, but now they were too big
to need that, and the mother began to introduce
grown-up ways of life. It was time to roost in
the trees. The young weasels, foxes, skunks,
and minks were beginning to run. The ground
grew more dangerous each night, so at sundown
Mother Partridge called ' *K-reet*,' and flew into
a thick, low tree.

The little ones followed, except one, an obsti-
nate little fool who persisted in sleeping on the
ground as heretofore. It was all right that
time, but the next night his brothers were
awakened by his cries. There was a slight
scuffle, then stillness, broken only by a horrid
sound of crunching bones and a smacking of
lips. They peered down into the terrible darkness below, where the glint of two close-set eyes

and a peculiar musty smell told them that a mink was the killer of their fool brother.

Six little partridges now sat in a row at night, with their mother in the middle, though it was not unusual for some little one with cold feet to perch on her back.

Their education went on, and about this time they were taught 'whirring.' A partridge can rise on the wing silently if it wishes, but whirring is so important at times that all are taught how and when to rise on thundering wings. Many ends are gained by the whirr. It warns all other partridges near that danger is at hand, it unnerves the gunner, or it fixes the foe's attention on the whirrer, while the others sneak off in silence, or by squatting, escape notice.

A partridge adage might well be 'foes and food for every moon.' September came, with seeds and grain in place of berries and ant-eggs, and gunners in place of skunks and minks.

The partridges knew well what a fox was, but had scarcely seen a dog. A fox they knew they could easily baffle by taking to a tree, but when in the Gunner Moon old Cuddy came prowling through the ravine with his bob-tailed

Redruff

yellow cur, the mother spied the dog and cried out, '*Kwit! kwit!*' (Fly, fly). Two of the brood thought it a pity their mother should lose her wits so easily over a fox, and were pleased to show their superior nerve by springing into a tree in spite of her earnestly repeated '*Kwit! kwit!*' and her example of speeding away on silent wings.

Meanwhile, the strange bob-tailed fox came under the tree and yapped and yapped at them. They were much amused at him and at their mother and brothers, so much so that they never noticed a rustling in the bushes till there was a loud *Bang! bang!* and down fell two bloody, flopping partridges, to be seized and mangled by the yellow cur until the gunner ran from the bushes and rescued the remains.

III

Cuddy lived in a wretched shanty near the Don, north of Toronto. His was what Greek philosophy would have demonstrated to be an ideal existence. He had no wealth, no taxes, no social pretensions, and no property to speak of. His life was made up of a very little work and a great deal of play, with as much out-door life as he chose. He considered himself a true sportsman because he was 'fond o' huntin',' and 'took a sight o' comfort out of seein' the critters hit the mud' when his gun was fired. The neighbors called him a squatter, and looked on him merely as an anchored tramp. He shot and trapped the year round, and varied his game somewhat with the season perforce, but had been heard to remark he could tell the month by the 'taste o' the patridges,' if he didn't happen to know by the almanac. This, no doubt, showed keen observation, but was also unfortunate proof of something not so creditable. The lawful season for murdering partridges began September 15th, but there was nothing surprising in Cuddy's being out a fortnight ahead of time. Yet he managed to escape punishment year after year, and even contrived to pose in a newspaper interview as an interesting character.

He rarely shot on the wing, preferring to pot his birds, which was not easy to do when the leaves were on, and accounted for the brood in

the third ravine going so long unharmed; but
the near prospect of other gunners finding them
now, had stirred him to go after 'a mess o'
birds.' He had heard no roar of wings when
the mother-bird led off her four survivors, so
pocketed the two he had killed and returned to
the shanty.

The little grouse thus learned that a dog is
not a fox, and must be differently played; and
an old lesson was yet more deeply graven—
' Obedience is long life.'

The rest of September was passed in keeping
quietly out of the way of gunners as well as
some old enemies. They still roosted on the
long thin branches of the hardwood trees among
the thickest leaves, which protected them from
foes in the air; the height saved them from foes
on the ground, and left them nothing to fear
but coons, whose slow, heavy tread on the lim-
ber boughs never failed to give them timely
warning. But the leaves were falling now—
every month its foes and its food. This was
nut time, and it was owl time, too. Barred
owls coming down from the north doubled or
trebled the owl population. The nights were

getting frosty and the coons less dangerous, so
the mother changed the place of roosting to the
thickest foliage of a hemlock-tree.

Only one of the brood disregarded the warning ' *Kreet, kreet.*' He stuck to his swinging
elm-bough, now nearly naked, and a great yel-
low-eyed owl bore him off before morning.

Mother and three young ones now were left,
but they were as big as she was ; indeed one,
the eldest, he of the chip, was bigger. Their
ruffs had begun to show. Just the tips, to tell
what they would be like when grown, and not
a little proud they were of them.

The ruff is to the partridge what the train is
to the peacock—his chief beauty and his pride.
A hen's ruff is black with a slight green gloss.
A cock's is much larger and blacker and is
glossed with more vivid bottle-green. Once in
a while a partridge is born of unusual size and
vigor, whose ruff is not only larger, but by
a peculiar kind of intensification is of a deep
coppery red, iridescent with violet, green, and
gold. Such a bird is sure to be a wonder to
all who know him, and the little one who had
squatted on the chip, and had always done what

he was told, developed before the Acorn Moon
had changed, into all the glory of a gold and
copper ruff—for this was Redruff, the famous
partridge of the Don Valley.

IV

One day late in the Acorn Moon, that is,
about mid-October, as the grouse family were
basking with full crops near a great pine log on
the sunlit edge of the beaver-meadow, they
heard the far-away bang of a gun, and Redruff,
acting on some impulse from within, leaped
on the log, strutted up and down a couple of
times, then, yielding to the elation of the
bright, clear, bracing air, he whirred his wings
in loud defiance. Then, giving fuller vent to
this expression of vigor, just as a colt frisks to
show how well he feels, he whirred yet more
loudly, until, unwittingly, he found himself
drumming, and tickled with the discovery of his
new power, thumped the air again and again till
he filled the near woods with the loud tattoo of
the fully grown cock-partridge. His brother
and sister heard and looked on with admiration

and surprise; so did his mother, but from that time she began to be a little afraid of him.

In early November comes the moon of a weird foe. By a strange law of nature, not wholly without parallel among mankind, all partridges go crazy in the November moon of their first year. They become possessed of a mad hankering to get away somewhere, it does not matter much where. And the wisest of them do all sorts of foolish things at this period. They go drifting, perhaps, at speed over the country by night, and are cut in two by wires, or dash into lighthouses, or locomotive head-lights. Daylight finds them in all sorts of absurd places, in buildings, in open marshes, perched on telephone wires in a great city, or even on board of coasting vessels. The craze seems to be a relic of a bygone habit of migra-tion, and it has at least one good effect, it breaks up the families and prevents the constant intermarrying, which would surely be fatal to their race. It always takes the young badly their first year, and they may have it again the second fall, for it is very catching; but in the third season it is practically unknown.

270

Redruff

Redruff's mother knew it was coming as soon as she saw the frost grapes blackening, and the maples shedding their crimson and gold. There was nothing to do but care for their health and keep them in the quietest part of the woods.

The first sign of it came when a flock of wild geese went *honking* southward overhead. The young ones had never before seen such long-necked hawks, and were afraid of them. But seeing that their mother had no fear, they took courage, and watched them with intense interest. Was it the wild, clanging cry that moved them, or was it solely the inner prompting then come to the surface? A strange longing to follow took possession of each of the young ones. They watched those arrowy trumpeters fading away to the south, and sought out higher perches to watch them farther yet, and from that time things were no more the same. The November moon was waxing, and when it was full, the November madness came.

The least vigorous of the flock were most affected. The little family was scattered. Redruff himself flew on several long erratic night journeys. The impulse took him southward,

271

Redruff

but there lay the boundless stretch of Lake Ontario, so he turned again, and the waning of the Mad Moon found him once more in the Mud Creek Glen, but absolutely alone.

V

Food grew scarce as winter wore on. Redruff clung to the old ravine and the piney sides of Taylor's Hill, but every month brought its food and its foes. The Mad Moon brought madness, solitude, and grapes; the Snow Moon came with rosehips; and the Stormy Moon brought browse of birch and silver storms that sheathed the woods in ice, and made it hard to keep one's perch while pulling off the frozen buds. Redruff's beak grew terribly worn with the work, so that even when closed there was still an opening through behind the hook. But nature had prepared him for the slippery footing; his toes, so slim and trim in September, had sprouted rows of sharp, horny points, and these grew with the growing cold, till the first snow had found him fully equipped with snow-shoes and ice-creepers. The cold weather had driven

272

Redruff

away most of the hawks and owls, and made
it impossible for his four-footed enemies to
approach unseen, so that things were nearly
balanced.

His flight in search of food had daily led him
farther on, till he had discovered and explored the
Rosedale Creek, with its banks of silver-birch,
and Castle Frank, with its grapes and rowan
berries, as well as Chester woods, where amel-
anchier and Virginia-creeper swung their fruit-
bunches, and checkerberries glowed beneath
the snow.

He soon found out that for some strange reason men with guns did not go within the high
fence of Castle Frank. So among these scenes
he lived his life, learning new places, new foods,
and grew wiser and more beautiful every day.

He was quite alone so far as kindred were
concerned, but that scarcely seemed a hardship.
Wherever he went he could see the jolly chickadees scrambling merrily about, and he remembered the time when they had seemed such
big, important creatures. They were the most
absurdly cheerful things in the woods. Before
the autumn was fairly over they had begun to

sing their famous refrain, '*Spring Soon*,' and kept it up with good heart more or less all

Shring ' soon

through the winter's direst storms, till at length the waning of the Hungry Moon, our February, seemed really to lend some point to the ditty, and they redoubled their optimistic announcement to the world in an ' I-told-you-so ' mood. Soon good support was found, for the sun gained strength and melted the snow from the southern slope of Castle Frank Hill, and exposed great banks of fragrant wintergreen, whose berries were a bounteous feast for Redruff, and, ending the hard work of pulling frozen browse, gave his bill the needed chance to grow into its proper shape again. Very soon the first bluebird came flying over and warbled as he flew ' *The spring is coming.*' The sun kept gaining, and early one day in the dark of the Wakening Moon of March there was a loud ' *Caw, caw,*' and old Silverspot, the king-

Redruff

crow, came swinging along from the south at the head of his troops and officially announced

'THE SPRING HAS COME.'

All nature seemed to respond to this, the opening of the birds' New Year, and yet it was something within that chiefly seemed to move them. The chickadees went simply wild; they sang their '*Spring now, spring now now—Spring now now,*' so persistently that one wondered how they found time to get a living.

And Redruff felt it thrill him through and through. He sprang with joyous vigor on a stump and sent rolling down the little valley, again and again, a thundering '*Thump, thump, thump, thunderrrrrrrr,*' that wakened dull echoes as it rolled, and voiced his gladness in the coming of the spring.

Away down the valley was Cuddy's shanty. He heard the drum-call on the still morning air and 'reckoned there was a cock patridge to git,' and came sneaking up the ravine with his gun. But Redruff skimmed away in silence, nor rested till once more in Mud Creek Glen. And there he mounted the very log where first he

275

had drummed and rolled his loud tattoo again
and again, till a small boy who had taken a short
cut to the mill through the woods, ran home,
badly scared, to tell his mother he was sure the
Indians were on the war-path, for he heard their
war-drums beating in the glen.

Why does a happy boy holla? Why does
a lonesome youth sigh? They don't know
any more than Redruff knew why every day
now he mounted some dead log and thumped
and thundered to the woods ; then strutted and
admired his gorgeous blazing ruffs as they
flashed their jewels in the sunlight, and then
thundered out again. Whence now came the
strange wish for someone else to admire the
plumes? And why had such a notion never
come till the Pussywillow Moon?

' *Thump, thump, thunder-r-r-r-r-r-rrrr* '
' *Thump, thump, thunder-r-r-r-r-r-rrrr* '
he rumbled again and again.

Day after day he sought the favorite log, and
a new beauty, a rose-red comb, grew out above
each clear, keen eye, and the clumsy snow-
shoes were wholly shed from his feet. His ruff
grew finer, his eye brighter, and his whole ap-

pearance splendid to behold, as he strutted and flashed in the sun. But—oh! he was *so lonesome now.*

Yet what could he do but blindly vent his hankering in this daily drum-parade, till on a day early in loveliest May, when the trilliums had fringed his log with silver stars, and he had drummed and longed, then drummed again, his keen ear caught a sound, a gentle footfall in the brush. He turned to a statue and watched; he knew he had been watched. Could it be possible? Yes! there it was—a form—another—a shy little lady grouse, now bashfully seeking to hide. In a moment he was by her side. His whole nature swamped by a new feeling—burnt up with thirst—a cooling spring in sight. And how he spread and flashed his proud array! How came he to know that that would please? He puffed his plumes and contrived to stand just right to catch the sun, and strutted and uttered a low, soft chuckle that must have been just as good as the 'sweet nothings' of another race, for clearly now her heart was won. Won, really, days ago, if only he had known. For full three days she had come at the loud tattoo and

coyly admired him from afar, and felt a little piqued that he had not yet found out her, so close at hand. So it was not quite all mischance, perhaps, that little stamp that caught his ear. But now she meekly bowed her head with sweet, submissive grace—the desert passed, the parch-burnt wanderer found the spring at last.

Oh, those were bright, glad days in the lovely glen of the unlovely name. The sun was never so bright, and the piney air was balmier sweet than dreams. And that great noble bird came daily on his log, sometimes with her and sometimes quite alone, and drummed for very joy of being alive. But why sometimes alone? Why not forever with his Brownie bride? Why should she stay to feast and play with him for hours, then take some stealthy chance to slip away and see him no more for hours or till next day, when his martial music from the log announced him restless for her quick return? There was a woodland mystery here he could not clear. Why should her stay with him grow daily less till it was down to minutes, and one day at last she never came at all. Nor the next, nor the next, and Redruff, wild, careered on lightning wing and drummed on the old log, then away up-stream on another log, and skimmed the hill to another ravine to drum and drum. But on the fourth day, when he came and loudly called her, as of old, at their earliest tryst, he heard a sound in the bushes, as at first, and there was his missing Brownie bride with ten little peeping partridges following after.

Redruff skimmed to her side, terribly frightening the bright-eyed downlings, and was just a little dashed to find the brood with claims far stronger than his own. But he soon accepted the change, and thenceforth joined himself to the brood, caring for them as his father never had for him.

VI

Good fathers are rare in the grouse world. The mother-grouse builds her nest and hatches out her young without help. She even hides the place of the nest from the father and meets him only at the drum-log and the feeding-ground, or perhaps the dusting-place, which is the club-house of the grouse kind.

When Brownie's little ones came out they had filled her every thought, even to the forgetting of their splendid father. But on the third day, when they were strong enough, she had taken them with her at the father's call.

Some fathers take no interest in their little ones, but Redruff joined at once to help Brownie in the task of rearing the brood. They had learned to eat and drink just as their father had learned long ago, and could toddle along, with their mother leading the way, while the father ranged near by or followed far behind.

The very next day, as they went from the hill-side down toward the creek in a somewhat drawn-out string, like beads with a big one at each end, a red squirrel, peeping around a pine-trunk, watched the procession of downlings with the Runtie straggling far in the rear. Redruff, yards behind, preening his feathers on a high log, had escaped the eye of the squirrel, whose strange perverted thirst for birdling blood was roused at what seemed so fair a chance. With murderous intent to cut off the hindmost straggler, he made a dash. Brownie could not have seen him until too late, but Redruff did. He flew for that red-haired cutthroat; his weapons were his fists, that is, the knob-joints of the wings, and what a blow he could strike! At the first onset he struck the squirrel square on the end of the nose, his weakest spot, and sent him reeling; he staggered and wriggled into a brush-pile, where he had expected to carry the little grouse, and there lay gasping with red drops trickling down his wicked snout. The partridges left him lying there, and what became of him they never knew, but he troubled them no more.

The family went on toward the water, but a cow had left deep tracks in the sandy loam, and into one of these fell one of the chicks and peeped in dire distress when he found he could not get out.

This was a fix. Neither old one seemed to know what to do, but as they trampled vainly round the edge, the sandy bank caved in, and, running down, formed a long slope, up which the young one ran and rejoined his brothers under the broad veranda of their mother's tail.

Brownie was a bright little mother, of small stature, but keen of wit and sense, and was, night and day, alert to care for her darling chicks. How proudly she stepped and clucked through the arching woods with her dainty brood behind her ; how she strained her little brown tail almost to a half-circle to give them a broader shade, and never flinched at sight of any foe, but held ready to fight or fly, whichever seemed the best for her little ones.

Before the chicks could fly they had a meeting with old Cuddy ; though it was June, he was out with his gun. Up the third ravine he went, and Tike, his dog, ranging ahead, came so dangerously near the Brownie brood that Redruff ran to meet him, and by the old but never failing trick led him on a foolish chase away back down the valley of the Don.

But Cuddy, as it chanced, came right along, straight for the brood, and Brownie, giving the signal to the children, '*Krrr, krrr*' (Hide, hide), ran to lead the man away just as her mate had led the dog. Full of a mother's devoted

love, and skilled in the learning of the woods,
she ran in silence till quite near, then sprang
with a roar of wings right in his face, and
tumbling on the leaves she shammed a lameness
that for a moment deceived the poacher. But
when she dragged one wing and whined about
his feet, then slowly crawled away, he knew just
what it meant—that it was all a trick to lead
him from her brood, and he struck at her a savage blow ; but little Brownie was quick, she
avoided the blow and limped behind a sapling,
there to beat herself upon the leaves again in
sore distress, and seem so lame that Cuddy
made another try to strike her down with a
stick. But she moved in time to balk him, and
bravely, steadfast still to lead him from her helpless little ones, she flung herself before him and
beat her gentle breast upon the ground, and
moaned as though begging for mercy. And
Cuddy, failing again to strike her, raised his
gun, and firing charge enough to kill a bear, he
blew poor brave, devoted Brownie into quiver-
ing, bloody rags.

This gunner brute knew the young must be
hiding near, so looked about to find them. But

no one moved or peeped. He saw not one, but
as he tramped about with heedless, hateful feet,
he crossed and crossed again their hiding-
ground, and more than one of the silent little
sufferers he trampled to death, and neither knew
nor cared.

Redruff had taken the yellow brute away off
down-stream, and now returned to where he
left his mate. The murderer had gone, taking
her remains, to be thrown to the dog. Redruff sought about and found the bloody spot
with feathers, Brownie's feathers, scattered
around, and now he knew the meaning of that
shot.

Who can tell what his horror and his mourn-
ing were? The outward signs were few, some
minutes dumbly gazing at the place with down-
cast, draggled look, and then a change at the
thought of their helpless brood. Back to the
hiding-place he went, and called the well-known
' *Kreet, kreet.*' Did every grave give up its little
inmate at the magic word? No, barely more than
half; six little balls of down unveiled their lus-
trous eyes, and, rising, ran to meet him, but four
feathered little bodies had found their graves in-

Redruff

deed. Redruff called again and again, till he was sure that all who could respond had come, then led them from that dreadful place, far, far away up-stream, where barb-wire fences and bramble thickets were found to offer a less grateful, but more reliable, shelter.

Here the brood grew and were trained by their father just as his mother had trained him; though wider knowledge and experience gave him many advantages. He knew so well the country round and all the feeding-grounds, and how to meet the ills that harass partridge-life, that the summer passed and not a chick was lost. They grew and flourished, and when the Gunner Moon arrived they were a fine family of six grown-up grouse with Redruff, splendid in his gleaming copper feathers, at their head. He had ceased to drum during the summer after the loss of Brownie, but drumming is to the partridge what singing is to the lark ; while it is his love-song, it is also an expression of exuberance born of health, and when the molt was over and September food and weather had renewed his splendid plumes and braced him up again, his spirits revived, and finding himself one day

285

near the old log he mounted impulsively, and drummed again and again.

From that time he often drummed, while his children sat around, or one who showed his father's blood would mount some nearby stump or stone, and beat the air in the loud tattoo.

The black grapes and the Mad Moon now came on. But Redruff's brood were of a vigorous stock; their robust health meant robust wits, and though they got the craze, it passed within a week, and only three had flown away for good.

Redruff, with his remaining three, was living in the glen when the snow came. It was light, flaky snow, and as the weather was not very cold, the family squatted for the night under the low, flat boughs of a cedar-tree. But next day the storm continued, it grew colder, and the drifts piled up all day. At night, the snow-fall ceased, but the frost grew harder still, so Redruff, leading the family to a birch-tree above a deep drift, dived into the snow, and the others did the same. Then into the holes the wind blew the loose snow—their pure white bed-clothes, and thus tucked in they slept in comfort, for the

Redruff

snow is a warm wrap, and the air passes through it easily enough for breathing. Next morning each partridge found a solid wall of ice before him from his frozen breath, but easily turned to one side and rose on the wing at Redruff's morning ' *Kreet, kreet, kwit.*' (Come children, come children, fly.)

This was the first night for them in a snow-drift, though it was an old story to Redruff, and next night they merrily dived again into bed, and the north wind tucked them in as before. But a change of weather was brewing. The night wind veered to the east. A fall of heavy flakes gave place to sleet, and that to silver rain. The whole wide world was sheathed in ice, and when the grouse awoke to quit their beds, they found themselves sealed in with a great cruel sheet of edgeless ice.

The deeper snow was still quite soft, and Redruff bored his way to the top, but there the hard, white sheet defied his strength. Hammer and struggle as he might he could make no impression, and only bruised his wings and head. His life had been made up of keen joys and dull hardships, with frequent sudden desperate

287

straits, but this seemed the hardest brunt of all, as the slow hours wore on and found him weakening with his struggles, but no nearer to freedom. He could hear the struggling of his family, too, or sometimes heard them calling to him for help with their long-drawn plaintive '*p-e-e-e-e-e-t-e, p-e-e-e-e-e-t-e.*'

They were hidden from many of their enemies, but not from the pangs of hunger, and when the night came down the weary prisoners, worn out with hunger and useless toil, grew quiet in despair. At first they had been afraid the fox would come and find them imprisoned there at his mercy, but as the second night went slowly by they no longer cared, and even wished he would come and break the crusted snow, and so give them at least a fighting chance for life.

But when the fox really did come padding over the frozen drift, the deep-laid love of life revived, and they crouched in utter stillness till he passed. The second day was one of driving storm. The north wind sent his snow-horses, hissing and careering over the white earth, tossing and curling their white manes

Redruff

and kicking up more snow as they dashed on. The long, hard grinding of the granular snow seemed to be thinning the snow-crust, for though far from dark below, it kept on growing lighter. Redruff had pecked and pecked at the under side all day, till his head ached and his bill was wearing blunt, but when the sun went down he seemed as far as ever from escape. The night passed like the others, except no fox went trotting overhead. In the morning he renewed his pecking, though now with scarcely any force, and the voices or struggles of the others were no more heard. As the daylight grew stronger he could see that his long efforts had made a brighter spot above him in the snow, and he continued feebly pecking. Outside, the storm-horses kept on trampling all day, the crust was really growing thin under their heels, and late that afternoon his bill went through into the open air. New life came with this gain, and he pecked away, till just before the sun went down he had made a hole that his head, his neck, and his ever-beautiful ruffs could pass. His great broad shoulders were too large, but he could now strike downward, which gave him

289

fourfold force ; the snow-crust crumbled quickly, and in a little while he sprang from his icy prison once more free. But the young ones! Redruff flew to the nearest bank, hastily gathered a few red hips to stay his gnawing hunger, then returned to the prison-drift and clucked and stamped. He got only one reply, a feeble '*peete, peete,*' and scratching with his sharp claws on the thinned granular sheet he soon broke through, and Graytail feebly crawled out of the hole. But that was all ; the others, scattered he could not tell where in the drift, made no reply, gave no sign of life, and he was forced to leave them. When the snow melted in the spring their bodies came to view, skin, bones, and feathers—nothing more.

VII

It was long before Redruff and Graytail fully recovered, but food and rest in plenty are sure cure-alls, and a bright clear day in midwinter had the usual effect of setting the vigorous Redruff to drumming on the log. Was it the drumming, or the tell-tale tracks of their snow-

shoes on the omnipresent snow, that betrayed
them to Cuddy? He came prowling again and
again up the ravine, with dog and gun, intent
to hunt the partridges down. They knew him
of old, and he was coming now to know them
well. That great copper-ruffed cock was be-
coming famous up and down the valley. During the Gunner Moon many a one had tried to
end his splendid life, just as a worthless wretch
of old sought fame by burning the Ephesian
wonder of the world. But Redruff was deep
in woodcraft. He knew just where to hide,
and when to rise on silent wing, and when to
squat till overstepped, then rise on thunder
wing within a yard to shield himself at once
behind some mighty tree-trunk and speed away.

But Cuddy never ceased to follow with his
gun that red-ruffed cock ; many a long snapshot
he tried, but somehow always found a tree, a
bank, or some safe shield between, and Redruff
lived and throve and drummed.

When the Snow Moon came he moved with
Graytail to the Castle Frank woods, where food
was plenty as well as grand old trees. There
was in particular, on the east slope among the

creeping hemlocks, a splendid pine.   It was six
feet through, and its first branches began at the
tops of the other trees.   Its top in summer-time
was a famous resort for the bluejay and his
bride.   Here, far beyond the reach of shot, in
warm spring days the jay would sing and dance
before his mate, spread his bright blue plumes
and warble the sweetest fairyland music, so
sweet and soft that few hear it but the one for
whom it is meant, and books know nothing at
all about it.

   This great pine had an especial interest for
Redruff, now living near with his remaining
young one, but its base, not its far-away crown,
concerned him.   All around were low, creeping hemlocks, and among them the partridge-
vine and the wintergreen grew, and the sweet
black acorns could be scratched from under the
snow.   There was no better feeding-ground,
for when that insatiable gunner came on them
there it was easy to run low among the hemlock
to the great pine, then rise with a derisive
whirr behind its bulk, and keeping the huge
trunk in line with the deadly gun, skim off in
safety.   A dozen times at least the pine had

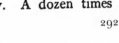

292

Redruff

saved them during the lawful murder season, and here it was that Cuddy, knowing their feeding habits, laid a new trap. Under the bank he sneaked and watched in ambush while an accomplice went around the Sugar Loaf to drive the birds. He came trampling through the low thicket where Redruff and Graytail were feeding, and long before the gunner was dangerously near Redruff gave a low warning '*rrr-rrr*' (danger) and walked quickly toward the great pine in case they had to rise.

Graytail was some distance up the hill, and suddenly caught sight of a new foe close at hand, the yellow cur, coming right on. Redruff, much farther off, could not see him for the bushes, and Graytail became greatly alarmed.

'*Kwit, kwit*' (Fly, fly), she cried, running down the hill for a start. '*Kreet, k-r-r-r*' (This way, hide), cried the cooler Redruff, for he saw that now the man with the gun was getting in range. He gained the great trunk, and behind it, as he paused a moment to call earnestly to Graytail, 'This way, this way,' he heard a slight noise under the bank before him that betrayed the ambush, then there was a ter-

rified cry from Graytail as the dog sprang at
her, she rose in air and skimmed behind the
shielding trunk, away from the gunner in the
open, right into the power of the miserable
wretch under the bank.

Whirr, and up she went, a beautiful, sen-
tient, noble being.

Bang, and down she fell—battered and bleeding, to gasp her life out and to lie a rumpled
mass of carrion in the snow.

It was a perilous place for Redruff. There was
no chance for a safe rise, so he squatted low.
The dog came within ten feet of him, and the
stranger, coming across to Cuddy, passed at
five feet, but he never moved till a chance came
to slip behind the great trunk away from both.
Then he safely rose and flew to the lonely glen
by Taylor's Hill.

One by one the deadly cruel gun had stricken
his near ones down, till now, once more, he
was alone. The Snow Moon slowly passed
with many a narrow escape, and Redruff, now
known to be the only survivor of his kind, was
relentlessly pursued, and grew wilder every day.

It seemed, at length, a waste of time to fol-

Redruff

low him with a gun, so when the snow was deepest, and food scarcest, Cuddy hatched a new plot. Right across the feeding-ground, almost the only good one now in the Stormy Moon, he set a row of snares. A cottontail rabbit, an old friend, cut several of these with his sharp teeth, but some remained, and Redruff, watching a far-off speck that might turn out a hawk, trod right in one of them, and in an instant was jerked into the air to dangle by one foot.

Have the wild things no moral or legal rights? What right has man to inflict such long and fearful agony on a fellow-creature, simply because that creature does not speak his language? All that day, with growing, racking pains, poor Redruff hung and beat his great, strong wings in helpless struggles to be free. All day, all night, with growing torture, until he only longed for death. But no one came. The morning broke, the day wore on, and still he hung there, slowly dying; his very strength a curse. The second night crawled slowly down, and when, in the dawdling hours of darkness, a great Horned Owl, drawn by the feeble flutter of a dying wing, cut short the pain, the deed was wholly kind.

The wind blew down the valley from the north. The snow-horses went racing over the wrinkled ice, over the Don Flats, and over the marsh toward the lake, white, for they were driven snow, but on them, scattered dark, were riding plumy fragments of partridge .ruffs—the famous rainbow ruffs. And they rode on the winter wind that night, away and away to the south, over the dark and boisterous lake, as they rode in the gloom of his Mad Moon flight, riding and riding on till they were engulfed, the last trace of the last of the Don Valley race.

For now no partridge comes to Castle Frank. Its woodbirds miss the martial spring salute, and in Mud Creek Ravine the old pine drum-log, since unused, has rotted in silence away.

A CATALOG OF SELECTED
DOVER BOOKS
IN ALL FIELDS OF INTEREST

A CATALOG OF SELECTED DOVER
BOOKS IN ALL FIELDS OF INTEREST

CONCERNING THE SPIRITUAL IN ART, Wassily Kandinsky. Pioneering work by father of abstract art. Thoughts on color theory, nature of art. Analysis of earlier masters. 12 illustrations. 80pp. of text. 5⅜ x 8½. 23411-8 Pa. $4.95

ANIMALS: 1,419 Copyright-Free Illustrations of Mammals, Birds, Fish, Insects, etc., Jim Harter (ed.). Clear wood engravings present, in extremely lifelike poses, over 1,000 species of animals. One of the most extensive pictorial sourcebooks of its kind. Captions. Index. 284pp. 9 x 12. 23766-4 Pa. $14.95

CELTIC ART: The Methods of Construction, George Bain. Simple geometric techniques for making Celtic interlacements, spirals, Kells-type initials, animals, humans, etc. Over 500 illustrations. 160pp. 9 x 12. (USO) 22923-8 Pa. $9.95

AN ATLAS OF ANATOMY FOR ARTISTS, Fritz Schider. Most thorough reference work on art anatomy in the world. Hundreds of illustrations, including selections from works by Vesalius, Leonardo, Goya, Ingres, Michelangelo, others. 593 illustrations. 192pp. 7⅛ x 10¼. 20241-0 Pa. $9.95

CELTIC HAND STROKE-BY-STROKE (Irish Half-Uncial from "The Book of Kells"): An Arthur Baker Calligraphy Manual, Arthur Baker. Complete guide to creating each letter of the alphabet in distinctive Celtic manner. Covers hand position, strokes, pens, inks, paper, more. Illustrated. 48pp. 8¼ x 11. 24336-2 Pa. $3.95

EASY ORIGAMI, John Montroll. Charming collection of 32 projects (hat, cup, pelican, piano, swan, many more) specially designed for the novice origami hobbyist. Clearly illustrated easy-to-follow instructions insure that even beginning papercrafters will achieve successful results. 48pp. 8¼ x 11. 27298-2 Pa. $3.50

THE COMPLETE BOOK OF BIRDHOUSE CONSTRUCTION FOR WOODWORKERS, Scott D. Campbell. Detailed instructions, illustrations, tables. Also data on bird habitat and instinct patterns. Bibliography. 3 tables. 63 illustrations in 15 figures. 48pp. 5¼ x 8½. 24407-5 Pa. $2.50

BLOOMINGDALE'S ILLUSTRATED 1886 CATALOG: Fashions, Dry Goods and Housewares, Bloomingdale Brothers. Famed merchants' extremely rare catalog depicting about 1,700 products: clothing, housewares, firearms, dry goods, jewelry, more. Invaluable for dating, identifying vintage items. Also, copyright-free graphics for artists, designers. Co-published with Henry Ford Museum & Greenfield Village. 160pp. 8¼ x 11. 25780-0 Pa. $10.95

HISTORIC COSTUME IN PICTURES, Braun & Schneider. Over 1,450 costumed figures in clearly detailed engravings–from dawn of civilization to end of 19th century. Captions. Many folk costumes. 256pp. 8⅜ x 11¾. 23150-X Pa. $12.95

THE INFLUENCE OF SEA POWER UPON HISTORY, 1660–1783, A. T. Mahan. Influential classic of naval history and tactics still used as text in war colleges. First paperback edition. 4 maps. 24 battle plans. 640pp. 5⅜ x 8½.　25509-3 Pa. $14.95

THE STORY OF THE TITANIC AS TOLD BY ITS SURVIVORS, Jack Winocour (ed.). What it was really like. Panic, despair, shocking inefficiency, and a little heroism. More thrilling than any fictional account. 26 illustrations. 320pp. 5⅜ x 8½.
20610-6 Pa. $8.95

FAIRY AND FOLK TALES OF THE IRISH PEASANTRY, William Butler Yeats (ed.). Treasury of 64 tales from the twilight world of Celtic myth and legend: "The Soul Cages," "The Kildare Pooka," "King O'Toole and his Goose," many more. Introduction and Notes by W. B. Yeats. 352pp. 5⅜ x 8½.　26941-8 Pa. $8.95

BUDDHIST MAHAYANA TEXTS, E. B. Cowell and Others (eds.). Superb, accurate translations of basic documents in Mahayana Buddhism, highly important in history of religions. The Buddha-karita of Asvaghosha, Larger Sukhavativyuha, more. 448pp. 5⅜ x 8½.　25552-2 Pa. $12.95

ONE TWO THREE . . . INFINITY: Facts and Speculations of Science, George Gamow. Great physicist's fascinating, readable overview of contemporary science: number theory, relativity, fourth dimension, entropy, genes, atomic structure, much more. 128 illustrations. Index. 352pp. 5⅜ x 8½.　25664-2 Pa. $8.95

ENGINEERING IN HISTORY, Richard Shelton Kirby, et al. Broad, nontechnical survey of history's major technological advances: birth of Greek science, industrial revolution, electricity and applied science, 20th-century automation, much more. 181 illustrations. ". . . excellent . . ."–*Isis*. Bibliography. vii + 530pp. 5⅜ x 8¼.
26412-2 Pa. $14.95

DALÍ ON MODERN ART: The Cuckolds of Antiquated Modern Art, Salvador Dalí. Influential painter skewers modern art and its practitioners. Outrageous evaluations of Picasso, Cézanne, Turner, more. 15 renderings of paintings discussed. 44 calligraphic decorations by Dalí. 96pp. 5⅜ x 8½. (USO)　29220-7 Pa. $4.95

ANTIQUE PLAYING CARDS: A Pictorial History, Henry René D'Allemagne. Over 900 elaborate, decorative images from rare playing cards (14th–20th centuries): Bacchus, death, dancing dogs, hunting scenes, royal coats of arms, players cheating, much more. 96pp. 9¼ x 12¼.　29265-7 Pa. $12.95

MAKING FURNITURE MASTERPIECES: 30 Projects with Measured Drawings, Franklin H. Gottshall. Step-by-step instructions, illustrations for constructing handsome, useful pieces, among them a Sheraton desk, Chippendale chair, Spanish desk, Queen Anne table and a William and Mary dressing mirror. 224pp. 8⅛ x 11¼.
29338-6 Pa. $13.95

THE FOSSIL BOOK: A Record of Prehistoric Life, Patricia V. Rich et al. Profusely illustrated definitive guide covers everything from single-celled organisms and dinosaurs to birds and mammals and the interplay between climate and man. Over 1,500 illustrations. 760pp. 7½ x 10⅛.　29371-8 Pa. $29.95

Prices subject to change without notice.

Available at your book dealer or write for free catalog to Dept. GI, Dover Publications, Inc., 31 East 2nd St., Mineola, N.Y. 11501. Dover publishes more than 500 books each year on science, elementary and advanced mathematics, biology, music, art, literary history, social sciences and other areas.